Shepherding a Child's Heart

Parent's Handbook

Shepherding a Child's Heart

Parent's Handbook

by Tedd Tripp

Shepherd Press
Wapwallopen, PA

Design and composition by Colophon Typesetting
Cover design by Now You See It!

Manufactured in the United States of America

*For the many couples I have met who love God
and desire to shepherd the hearts of their children*

Contents

Preface

It is a joy to introduce *Shepherding a Child's Heart: Parent's Handbook.* In the five years since the publication of *Shepherding a Child's Heart,* I have had the opportunity to teach on child rearing to hundreds of young parents across the country and in many other parts of the world. This effort, through the *Parent's Handbook,* to deepen the material in *Shepherding a Child's Heart* flows from that experience.

Teaching thousands of young parents in hundreds of seminars, listening to their questions and sharing their life experience has focused the content of this *Parent's Handbook.* I have gained a sharper focus on both the conceptual and cultural challenges confronting parents who are earnest about shepherding the hearts of their children.

As I have had five more years to think about this topic, many insights and Scriptural applications have come to mind. One of the joys of Bible study is that one never plumbs the depths of the Word of God; there are always new implications and applications of rich biblical truth. If I were writing *Shepherding a Child's Heart* today, the truths in the book could be more fully developed through insights I have gained in the past five years.

I had originally planned to call this book a study guide, but as I worked on it and it began to take shape I realized that it was really a parent's handbook. While it is designed to be used alongside *Shepherding a Child's Heart,* it does more than simply rehearse the material in the book. It will lead you into deeper understanding of the biblical concepts that are spelled out in *Shepherding.* If you, like so many, have desired to gain a richer and deeper understanding of the scriptural call to shepherding your child's heart, then I offer this *Parent's Handbook* as a way to strengthen your grasp of biblical principles of child rearing.

May God bless your faithful nurture of your children and raise up from our homes a holy seed for his church.

Tedd Tripp

January 2001

How to Use This Book

Shepherding a Child's Heart: Parent's Handbook is unusual, so some explanation is in order. I did not want to write a fill-in-the-blank study guide that simply rehearsed the material in the book. What I have sought to do is deepen the content and application of *Shepherding a Child's Heart*. Many of the questions in this book are not about the content of *Shepherding a Child's Heart*, but rather about the meaning and application of Scripture texts to the challenges of shepherding children.

Here is what you will find inside.

THE BIG IDEA   This section is simply a summary of the portion of *Shepherding a Child's Heart* that is under discussion. In each case the appropriate chapters from *Shepherding* are noted.

DIGGING INTO THE WORD   Here I have provided many passages of Scripture that will provide insight and understanding as you seek to understand your parenting task. The questions in this section are designed to direct your thinking and reasoning through the passages under examination.

APPLICATION   This section does exactly what the name implies; it leads into application of the biblical principles and concepts that bear on your parenting task.

STRATEGIC QUESTIONS   These questions are designed to help parents commit to change in any areas in which change would make them more biblical, Christ-centered parents. This section is designed to help you avoid the frequent problem of gaining insight without ever making the life changing decisions that move insight into lifestyle.

CONCLUDING THOUGHTS   This is the "where do I find the strength to do this" section. In each concluding thoughts segment I have sought to encourage parents from the scriptures that all the strength, all the insight, all the stamina, all the power, all the grace, all the courage, indeed all that you need to be what God has called you to be, has been given to you in Christ (2 Peter 1:2–4).

I believe that the *Parent's Handbook* will be useful for several applications. It will have value for personal study as a means of deepening the grasp of the principles in *Shepherding a Child's Heart*. It will be of great value for Sunday school or small group study purposes. It will provide some with a reason to study *Shepherding* all over again. It will be of help to a study leader who is looking for greater depth of understanding.

However you choose to use it, I pray Paul's prayer for you:

> And this is my prayer: that your love may abound more and more in knowledge and depth of insight, so that you may be able to discern what is best and may be pure and blameless until the day of Christ, filled with the fruit of righteousness that comes through Jesus Christ—to the glory and praise of God.   *Philippians 1:9–11*

Shepherding a Child's Heart

Parent's Handbook

CHAPTER 1

Getting to the
Heart of Behavior

THE BIG IDEA

The heart is the control center of life. All behavior flows from the heart. This is why Jesus says, "For out of the overflow of his heart his mouth speaks." (Luke 6:45). What comes out in the words and actions of your children reflect the abundance of their hearts. Correction and discipline, therefore, must be concerned with heart issues. Your concern is to unmask your child's sin, helping him to understand how it reflects a heart that has strayed. Correction provides opportunities to show the glories of God who sent His Son to change hearts and free people enslaved to sin.

This chapter discusses the information found in Chapter 1 of *Shepherding a Child's Heart*.

DIGGING INTO THE WORD

1. God is concerned with heart issues. Make notes on the following passages. How do they show God's focus on the heart?

Proverbs 4:23 _____

_____

Deuteronomy 10:12 _____

_____

Jeremiah 17:10 _____

_____

Luke 12:34 _____

_____

2. To shepherd your child's heart into a biblical understanding of behavior, you must know the terms the Bible
   uses to describe the thoughts and purposes of the heart.
   Look up and write out Hebrews 4:12.

   _____

   _____

   _____

   _____

3. The Bible is robust and sufficient. It gives you all the categories of thought you need to understand and evaluate
   behavior. From the list of Scripture texts below identify
   the heart issues that inevitably lead to sin.

Romans 12:19 _____

Proverbs 29:25 _____

Psalm 10:4_____

Psalm 56:3,4,11 _____

Deuteronomy 7:25 _____

Ecclesiastes 4:4_____

Proverbs 10:12_____

James 3:14,16 _____

Psalm 17:10 _____

Acts 5:17 _____

1 Corinthians 3:1,3 _____

1 Corinthians 10:14_____

Romans 3:14_____

The passages listed above are only suggestive, not exhaustive. Develop a notebook in which you collect the attitudes of heart that the Bible uses to describe things that motivate behavior. Write the texts that describe these heart attitudes. Think of stories in the Scripture that can illustrate these character qualities both positively and negatively. Show how they work out in the lives of Bible characters. Hezekiah, for example, could be enlisted as an illustration of pride.

Look at the list of heart attitudes above and think of biblical terms that describe the opposite quality. For example, opposite hatred, place love. In your notebook generate a list of contrasting attitudes of heart. Train yourself and your children to think and speak of motivation using biblical terminology.

When we assign terms to heart attitudes that are not biblical terms, we move our thinking away from the Bible as a means of understanding our motives and attitudes. For example, what does a person mean when he describes himself as frustrated? Does he mean angry, or something different? No passages of Scripture speak to frustration because it is not a biblical term. Until we identify those feelings with biblical terminology, we cannot use the Bible to understand them.

The purpose for describing the attitudes of heart that motivate behavior is *not to assign motives* to your child with greater precision. Never use these insights from Scripture to club your child with his failure and inner wickedness. The reason to hone your understanding of these biblical terms is to enable you to help your child understand how the Scriptures describe the things that motivate what he says and does. You are using your knowledge to increase his sensitivity to and understanding of what pushes and pulls his behavior.

Your task is to explore with your child the possible motives for his actions and to help him to learn to discern what is going on within. Your integrity in dealing with these issues of motivation in your own life will both give you insight and credibility as you seek to deal with these things in your children. You can never teach what you have not learned.

APPLICATION

1. What are some of the reasons you get sidetracked with behavior?

_____

_____

_____

_____

2. Why is changed behavior not an adequate goal in correction?

_____

_____

_____

3. Note what these passages say about behavior change that is not tied to heart change.

Matthew 15:8 _____

_____

Matthew 23:25–28 _____

_____

4. How does understanding that behavior is only a reflection
    of the attitudes of the heart change the focus in correc-
    tion and discipline?

_____

_____

_____

_____

_____

5. Focusing on behavior rather than on the heart has nega-
    tive results. Focus on changing behavior will tempt you to
    become a behaviorist. Behaviorism is the attempt to con-
    trol or constrain behavior through offering negative or
    positive consequences. What are some of the things you
    have done to change behavior without focusing on heart
    issues?

_____

_____

_____

_____

_____

There are times when you must constrain behavior. For example, if your son is hitting his sister on the head with a baseball bat, you must constrain his behavior. You cannot wait for
his heart to change. The behavior must be stopped. But, even

when you require him to stop hurting his sister in that way, you do so in the knowledge that the problem is not necessarily addressed just because the wrong behavior has stopped. You must still explore with him the heart issues behind this wrong behavior that requires restraint.

Remember, in correction and discipline, you are interested in what is happening in the heart. How has the heart has gone astray? Concern for heart issues leads to the cross of Christ. Concern for heart issues underscores the need for a Savior. It provides you with opportunities to point your children to the willing, able, powerful Savior of sinners. He is the only One who does heart transplant surgery. He removes hearts of stone and implants hearts of flesh. (Ezekiel 36:26).

STRATEGIC QUESTIONS

1. What are some of the ways that you have been a behaviorist rather than a shepherd of the heart of your child?

   _____

   _____

   _____

   _____

2. In what ways would identifying the thoughts and intents of the heart help you to correct and discipline with a more Christ centered focus?

   _____

   _____

   _____

   _____

3. What questions can you develop (questions that cannot be answered "yes" or "no") that will help you draw your children out in ways that focus correction and discipline on heart issues?

_____

_____

_____

_____

_____

4. What changes in your style of interacting with correction and discipline would help you to apply the ideas in this chapter?

_____

_____

5. How should your goals in correction and discipline change?

_____

_____

6. How do you need to apply these truths to your life in order to move toward your children with integrity and insight?

_____

_____

_____

7. What are some ways that you must pray for yourself and
    your children if you are to apply these things to your cor-
    rection, discipline and motivation of your children?

    _____

    _____

    _____

    _____

CONCLUDING THOUGHTS

You know that you are on the right track when you are trying
to understand the thoughts and the motives of the heart, because this is one of the primary functions of the Bible.

> For the word of God is living and active. Sharper than any
> double-edged sword, it penetrates even to dividing soul and
> spirit, joints and marrow; it judges the thoughts and attitudes
> of the heart.   *Hebrews 4:12*

One of the implications of this passage is that you must
know the Scriptures. Unless the Word of God dwells richly in
you, you will be ineffective in using it as a means of helping
your children understand the overflow of their hearts.

1. Hebrews 4:12 raises this question: What are the thoughts
    and attitudes of your heart in correction and discipline?
    Make a list of wrong thoughts and attitudes of heart that
    may divert and confuse your focus in the discipline, cor-
    rection and motivation of your children.

    _____

    _____

_____

_____

_____

_____

_____

_____

_____

2. The temptation when you are confronted with penetrat-
    ing issues from the Bible is to become discouraged and
    think that we can never learn to do these things, or that
    it will be too little, too late, or that perhaps your children
    are too hard. Whatever the temptation that you face, you
    may be assured of God's power and strength to bring
    change.

    What phrases in the verses below fill you with joy, hope
    and courage as you strive to provide biblical structures of
    discipline for your children?

Ephesians 3:20_____

_____

2 Peter 1:3–4_____

_____

2 Chronicles 16:9_____

_____

Psalm 139:23–24_____

_____

_____

Since God has given us His Word to be a means of understanding the thoughts and attitudes of the heart, you are in sync with God's objectives as you strive to understand the overflow of the heart issues in correction and discipline. You may be assured of His help and grace as you shepherd the hearts of your children.

CHAPTER 2

Shaping Influences and Godward Orientation

THE BIG IDEA

Two things contribute to the development of your child: the shaping influences of life and the Godward orientation of his heart. As a parent you must be concerned with both. You must be concerned with how you structure the shaping influences of life under your control. You must also actively shepherd the Godward orientation of your children. Your children are not neutral in this process. They are not merely the sum total of what you put into them. They interact with your shaping efforts according the Godward commitment of their hearts. Raising children is not like operating a plastic extrusion press. Children are responders. They are active in what they become.

This chapter discusses the information found in chapters 2 & 3 of *Shepherding a Child's Heart*.

DIGGING INTO THE WORD

Shaping Influences

1. In the following passages look for evidence of God's concern with the shaping influences you provide for your children.

Genesis 18:19 _____

_____

Deuteronomy 6:6–9_____

_____

Ephesians 6:4 _____

_____

Colossians 3:21_____

_____

2. How would you summarize the importance God places on
    the shaping influences you provide as a parent?

_____

_____

_____

3. Notice in the following passages the effect of shaping in-
    fluences on children.

Proverbs 1:8–9 _____

_____

Proverbs 3:1–2 _____

_____

Proverbs 23:19_____

_____

Proverbs 23:22_____

_____

Proverbs 23:26 _____

_____

Proverbs 29:21 _____

_____

Godward Orientation

1. The Bible speaks with clarity as it describes the importance
    of the Godward orientation of your child's heart. In the
    following passages look for evidences of the importance
    of Godward orientation in determining how your children
    will respond to life and life's circumstances.

Genesis 50:19–21 _____

_____

Psalm 10:1–11 _____

_____

Psalm 14:11 _____

_____

Proverbs 4:23 _____

_____

Proverbs 9:7–10 _____

_____

Mark 7:21–23 _____

_____

Luke 6:45_____

_____

Romans 1:21–25 _____

_____

2. 1 Samuel 2:12, provides a good case study in the importance of Godward orientation. "Eli's sons were wicked men;
   they had no regard for the Lord. . ." Everything in the rest
   of the story is an outworking of the Godward orientation
   of the hearts of these wicked sons of Eli. The ways they
   sinned in the account we are given in 1 Samuel were
   merely a reflection of the Godward orientation of their
   hearts; they had no regard for the Lord.

   How would you summarize the importance of the Godward orientation of your child's heart?

   _____

   _____

   _____

   _____

3. Begin looking for passages and illustrations that demonstrate the importance of providing good shaping influences in areas in where you have some control and input.
   Also gather Bible illustrations of how the Godward orientation of the heart determines response to life's circumstances. Here are some examples to get you started.

   A. In Ephesians 6:4, God shows how He is concerned with
      the shaping influences provided by a father. The im-
      plication is that children will become embittered by im-
      proper parental control.

   B. In 1 Peter 2:13–23, the entrusting of one's self to God
      (v. 23) determines how to respond to the experience
      of being punished unfairly.

C. Psalm 3:1–6 shows how confidence in God enables David to find rest even when an army is against him. Godward orientation changes the way that situation is experienced by the Psalmist.

Most discussions of child rearing are discussions of providing the best possible shaping influences. There is a certain value in this because, as you see in the Scripture, the shaping influences of life have a powerful impact on your children's lives. Many shaping influences, however, are not under parental control. Some things such as sickness, death, social and cultural movements come to us according to God's plan without regard to our preferences. The shaping influences that we can control must be structured according to God's Word. You must teach your children to respond to those things you cannot control with an understanding of God and His ways.

APPLICATION

1. As you see in the passages you looked at above, the shaping influences of life have an impact on your children. It is, therefore, valid for you to be concerned with the shaping influences that you have some control over.

    Evaluate with your spouse the shaping influences you are providing in these areas. Ask yourself what passages of Scripture speak to these things.

Family worship _____

Conflict resolution_____

Family values _____

Roles of father or mother_____

Success and failure_____

Importance of serving others_____

Fellowship_____

Importance of education _____

Development of talents_____

Decision making_____

Character development_____

Place of the Bible_____

2. Chapter 2 of *Shepherding a Child's Heart* describes two mistakes that can be made in understanding the parenting task—determinism or denial. Review that section and respond to the following questions.

   A. How would determinism affect the way you would respond to your child rearing task?

   _____

   _____

   _____

   B. How would denial affect the way you would respond to your child rearing task?

   _____

   _____

   _____

   C. How do you see yourself responding either in determinism or denial?

   _____

   _____

_____

_____

The shaping influences of life and the Godward orientation of the hearts of your children both contribute to the persons they become. The Bible teaches that, "If a man pampers his servant from youth, he will bring grief in the end." (Proverbs 29:21). The shaping influence of pampering will bring the result of an unworthy servant who will be a grief to his master. Shaping influences matter. They have an impact on how a servant develops. Likewise, the Godward orientation of the heart will impact the person our child becomes. The shaping influences are never the sole determiner because the Godward orientation of the heart directs the way the individual responds to what happens to him in his life experience. Certainly, Joseph is an example of one who trusted God and understood life from the perspective of God's sovereign control, despite the difficult shaping influences in his life (see Gen 50:20).

3. What do you discern to be the ways your child is responding to his life experience? Do you see him responding in love for God and faith in God's care and goodness, or do you see him pushed and pulled by other things?

_____

_____

_____

4. What are some of the ways he shows that he is responding to life as a child who knows and loves God or as a child who is still quite willful and bent on pleasing himself?

_____

_____

_____

5. If you use Proverbs 9:7–10 as a grid through which to understand your child's response to the direction and correction he receives from you, would you characterize him as wise or as a mocker?

    _____

    _____

6. If as a wise person, how can you encourage and strengthen those wise responses?

    _____

    _____

7. If as a mocker, how can you challenge and demonstrate the destructiveness of those foolish responses?

    _____

    _____

8. While you cannot control all the shaping influences, you can shepherd the hearts of your children as they respond to these things. How could you shepherd the heart of your child in the following situations? (Assume for the moment, that you cannot change the situation).

    A. There is an art teacher that seems to respond unfairly to your child. How can you help him to understand this trial in a biblical vision?

        _____

        _____

        _____

        _____

B. There is a bully on the school bus who sees your child's gracious responses as weakness and has become a daily tormentor to your child. Help him respond to this in a godly manner.

_____

_____

_____

_____

C. Daddy is sick. In fact, he is dying and life must be organized around his needs and hospice care. How could you shepherd your child to know God and peace and comfort in this life experience?

_____

_____

_____

_____

Many parents show far more concern for the shaping influences of life than they show for the Godward orientation of their child's heart as he responds to those shaping influences. It is far more important, for example, to shepherd the response your child has to the bully at school than it is to insure that no one ever bullies him. Whether people laugh at your child is of little import compared with learning to know God in ways that enable him to respond to the experience of being laughed at.

Your child is never neutral as he responds to the shaping influences of life. He is a creature who was made in the image of God. He is uniquely designed to know God and be dazzled by God's glory. Because he is a worshiper, he will always respond to life out of a religious grid. Your task is twofold. First, to provide the most biblical shaping influences you can provide. Second, to shepherd his heart through all of life's hills and valleys into the paths of intimate communion and fellowship with God.

STRATEGIC QUESTIONS

1. What are ways that you need to rethink aspects of the shaping influences that you provide for your children?

   _____

   _____

   _____

2. What are some changes that you should make in order to have the shaping influences that you provide be more consistently biblical?

   _____

   _____

   _____

3. Children either respond to life out of the grace of God's covenant and know his peace and joy, or they respond with some form of idolatry such as pride and performance, power and influence, pleasure and sensuality or perhaps love of possessions. What do you observe as the lens through which your children are looking at the world?

   _____

   _____

   _____

4. Can you think of ways to open discussion with them about these issues?

_____

_____

_____

5. What are some ways that you must pray for yourself and for your children if you are going to apply these things to the correction and discipline of your children?

_____

_____

_____

CONCLUDING THOUGHTS

One of the ways that God causes us to grow in grace and knowing Him is prayerful self-reflection. Meditate on the shaping influences of life that are under your control. Prayerfully evaluate areas of needed change. Think about the need to show your children the excellencies and glories of God. Then open your heart before God with the words of Psalm 26:2–3: "Test me, O LORD, and try me, examine my heart and my mind; for your love is ever before me, and I walk continually in your truth."

1. What are some ways the shaping influences of life under your control should be changed?

_____

_____

2. How can you deepen your experience of the pleasures of knowing God, so that you can reflect to your children in

deeper measure the joys of communion and fellowship with the living God?

One of the most powerful ways that you can show your children the glories of God, whose greatness no one can fathom, is by finding delight in Him yourself. As you delight in Him and show His wonders to your children, you bring Him glory. Look up Psalm 145 as a paradigm of the excellencies of God.

The promises of the Scripture were given to encourage us.

> For everything that was written in the past was written to teach us, so that through endurance and the encouragement of the Scriptures we might have hope. *Romans 15:4*

As you give yourself to painful self-examination and strive to change in the ways that God calls you to for the sake of raising your children, fortify your heart with the encouragements of Scripture.

God will draw near to us and show himself strong as we seek to change.

> I pray that out of his glorious riches he may strengthen you with power through his Spirit in your inner being, so that Christ may dwell in your hearts through faith. And I pray that you, being rooted and established in love, may have power, together with all the saints, to grasp how wide and long and

high and deep is the love of Christ, and to know this love that surpasses knowledge—that you may be filled to the measure of all the fullness of God. Now to him who is able to do immeasurably more than all we ask or imagine, according to his power that is at work within us, to him be glory in the church and in Christ Jesus throughout all generations, for ever and ever! Amen.   *Ephesians 3:16–21*

3. Note all the encouragements in the passage above that fill you with hope, joy and courage as you give yourself to what God calls you to.

CHAPTER 3

You're in Charge

THE BIG IDEA

God has established structures of authority. The essential social structures of life—the home, the church, and the state—all have God-ordained authorities. Parents are the God-ordained authority in the lives of children. Your children need the gracious authority of parents, who know them and who understand God's ways. Children lack maturity, wisdom and life experience. They thrive under the gracious authority of godly parents. Our culture does not like authority. It is not just that we don't like being under authority, we don't like being authorities. Hence, many parents are uncomfortable with their calling to be authorities in their children's lives. Their discomfort with authority makes them tentative and insecure with their authority over their children. In a biblical vision, we understand that God calls parents to be authorities and has ordained that living under parental authority is a blessing for our children. (Ephesians 6:1–3).

This chapter discusses the information in Chapter 4 of *Shepherding a Child's Heart.*

DIGGING INTO THE WORD

God calls parents to be authorities in the lives of their children. Look at the passages listed below. Note the implications in terms of parental authority.

Genesis 18:19 _____

_____

Deuteronomy 21:18–21 _____

_____

Proverbs 1:8–9 _____

_____

Proverbs 4:1–2 _____

_____

Proverbs 6:20–23 _____

_____

Proverbs 23:22 _____

_____

Luke 2:51–52 _____

_____

Ephesians 6:1–4 _____

_____

Colossians 3:20–21 _____

_____

1 Thessalonians 2:11–12_____

_____

1. Our culture has reduced parenting to care providing. What would be some tasks that could be listed as care providing tasks?

_____

_____

_____

2. What additional callings does Chapter 4 of *Shepherding a Child's Heart* remind us of?

_____

_____

_____

APPLICATION

As we have observed above, in our culture we do not like authority. We do not like being under authority, nor do we like being authorities. Requiring someone to obey us seems unfair to us. To love someone and to require them to obey seems strange in our time. We would rather have our children do what we want without having to require it of them. As a result, many parents are uncomfortable with teaching children to submit to authority. Young children grow accustomed to making their own decisions.

> Honey, do you really think you should wear that pink party dress and those patent leather shoes to the picnic?

> Wouldn't it be better for you to wear your jeans and a pair of sneakers?

> OK, but I hope you don't spoil your nice dress. Don't come crying to me if it gets messed up.

And so young Jennifer is the decision-maker. She may be too young and lack the maturity to make a good decision, but she has become the decision-maker. Here are the sad results.

She is learning that parents may suggest, but she has the final say. She is learning to be an autonomous person who has no greater authority in her life than her own wishes and desires. She is learning to trust her own ideas and to resist the counsel and direction of parents who are mature and wise.

> I'm sorry, Mommy forgot that you don't like oatmeal. Look, you don't have to eat it. What would you like to eat? How about some cocoa pops? I'll get the cocoa pops.

Would it not be better for Junior and for Mother if Mother said, "Dear, I know that oatmeal is not your favorite cereal, but Mommy made oatmeal this morning. It is good nutritious food and I want you to eat it. Now, let's pray and thank God for the food He has given us. Maybe we will have something you like better another day."

What is Junior learning? He is learning that Mommy is in charge. She is an authority who is kind. He is learning to give thanks in all circumstances. He is learning that the adults in his world are not going to act like peers; they will act like adults. He is learning to be under the authority of someone older, wiser and more mature.

1. What are some areas in which you observe parents being unwilling to provide direction for their children?

_____

_____

_____

Scores of scenarios likes these above could be played out. Discussions about piano lessons, T-ball teams, ballet classes, sleepovers, having friends in, visiting other friends or neighbors and so forth could be described. The point is this: your task in dealing with young children is to determine what is best for your child and direct him into that path in kind and gracious ways. You must provide direction.

Your children are young. They lack maturity, wisdom and life experience. They need the direction and protection of kind and gentle parents who are willing to be in charge. When we fail to provide this direction we imply that they do not need us for direction. Once we have taught them that lesson (through failure to direct) we will find it very hard to persuade them differently.

It is important to present this lesson of being a person under authority in positive ways. "Honey, God, who is good and kind and who has made you and me and all things for His glory, says that boys and girls are to obey their Mommy and Daddy. God loves you so much that He has given you a Mommy and Daddy who are wise and love you and care for you. It is a good thing for you to obey Mommy and Daddy."

2. In addition to providing direction, parents must also discipline. What are some mistaken notions some parents have about discipline?

   _____

   _____

   _____

3. Read the description of discipline in Hebrews 12:5–11. What is the difference between a punitive and a corrective view of discipline?

   _____

   _____

   _____

4. Why is it important that correction orbit around a God who has been sinned against and not a parent who is offended?

_____

_____

_____

_____

_____

5. How does correcting because of offense toward God help with the problem of parental anger during discipline?

_____

_____

_____

_____

_____

6. How will seeing yourself as God's agent in correction and discipline change the way you discipline your children?

_____

_____

_____

_____

_____

Meditate on the implications of Proverbs 3:11–12: "My son, do not despise the Lord's discipline and do not resent his rebuke, because the LORD disciplines those he loves, as a father the son he delights in."

STRATEGIC QUESTIONS

1. What are some ways that you fail in being an authority and fall to negotiating with your children rather than directing them?

   _____

   _____

   _____

2. Are you perhaps a parent who does not struggle with being an authority, but who struggles with being an authority who is kind? How can you exhibit the Christ-like gentleness of Matthew 11:29–30?

   _____

   _____

   _____

   _____

3. You are to be obeyed because you are God's agent for discipline and correction. Your authority is derived from God's authority. It is easy to become muddled in your thinking and to cease to see yourself as an authority under God and to just want to be obeyed out of personal convenience. What are the ways that this all reduces to convenience for you and the issue becomes simply wanting what you want?

   _____

   _____

   _____

   _____

3. How can you present to your children the benefits of being a person under authority?

_____

_____

_____

_____

4. What are the truths that they need to embrace if they are to find joy in being a person under the authority of their parents?

_____

_____

_____

_____

5. Think about non-corrective contexts (when you are not in the process of confronting improper behavior and attitudes in your children) in which you can present truths your children must understand and affirm in order to submit to God's order and be under authority. What are some of the truths you must teach?

_____

_____

_____

_____

_____

_____

6. You know that God has called you to be an authority in the lives of your children. You want to be an authority that is kind. What are some areas in which you must grow in grace to be a gracious and godly authority in the lives of your children?

_____

_____

_____

_____

_____

7. What qualities do you find in God that you can imitate in being a gracious authority in the lives of your children?

_____

_____

_____

CONCLUDING THOUGHTS

1. The parenting task often seems overwhelming. You must deal with yourself and the problems of habit and personality that you bring to the task. You also must deal with children, each of whom bring certain proclivities and ways of thinking and responding to the parent-child relationship. You stand in continual need of the grace and strength of Jesus Christ. Only in Him can you find the strength, insight, wisdom and hope you need to do this task with joy. Note how these passages express biblical hope.

Isaiah 41:10 _____

_____

_____

2 Chronicles 7:14 _____

_____

_____

John 15:3–5 _____

_____

_____

2. Make a prayer list of ways you can pray for yourself and your spouse as you seek to be kind authorities in the lives of your children. How do you need the grace of God that comes as you abide in the vine? What are the ways that your children need God's work in them if they are to be children who willingly place themselves under your authority?

_____

_____

_____

_____

_____

_____

_____

_____

We are a culture that does not understand authority in a biblical vision. We tend toward being wimps or being John Wayne type authorities. God, who is working in us, will give us grace to be Christ-like authorities like the One who said, "Come to me, all you who are weary and burdened, and I will give you rest. Take my yoke upon you and learn from me, for I am gentle and humble in heart, and you will find rest for your souls. For my yoke is easy and my burden is light." (Matthew 11:28–30).

CHAPTER 4

Establishing Your Goals

THE BIG IDEA

Life at the turn of the century confronts us with a dizzying array of things to do with and for our children. Children's teams and leagues are formed for baseball, football, soccer, hockey, swimming, dance classes and gymnastics, to only name a few. There are educational opportunities; we know we want them ready to live in the information age (even if we aren't quite sure what the information age is). In addition to all this, we are tempted to fill our children's lives with material things. And we take delight in their delight in possessions. We take them to the thriller movies providing them with large doses of adrenaline as they vicariously experience the superhero's life and death adventures. Somehow we believe that our task as parents is to be activity directors who keep our children from ever feeling bored. We forget that the chief end of man is to glorify God and enjoy Him forever. Successful parenting isn't filling our children's lives with activities and possessions, it is teaching them that it is only in His light that we see light. The living God is the only true delight of the soul. Only in Him will our thirst be sated.

This chapter discusses the information in Chapters 5 and 6 of *Shepherding a Child's Heart*.

DIGGING INTO THE WORD

Children, indeed all human beings, are made for God. We are made for relationship with Him. We are made to know God and live in a relationship of communion and fellowship with Him. Make note of the ways these passages describe the pleasures of knowing God.

Psalm 4:6–7 _____

_____

Psalm 16:2 & 11 _____

_____

Psalm 36:5–9_____

_____

Psalm 42:1–2_____

_____

Psalm 63:1–8_____

_____

Isaiah 55:1–2_____

_____

These passages and many others show that life is found in the joys and delightful pleasures of knowing and loving God. As Augustine said long ago, "We are restless until our souls find their rest in Him."

1. How many ways can you list that parents unwittingly offer alternate pleasures and joys that distract their children from knowing God?

_____

_____

_____

_____

_____

_____

_____

2. Throughout the Scriptures we read of God's concern that His people not be influenced by the standards and values of the nations around them. Goals for child rearing are one of the places where the standards and values of the culture around us have their greatest impact on the people of God. Identify the ways these passages warn against the influences of the culture around us.

Colossians 2:8_____

_____

Ephesians 5:8–10 _____

_____

Leviticus 20:26_____

_____

Deuteronomy 18:9–10_____

_____

The passage above from Deuteronomy is shocking because we cannot imagine sacrificing our sons and daughters in a fire. May I suggest that we do exactly that when we turn them over to the coaches and teachers so they "learn to imitate the detestable ways of the nations". When our sons learn to play football from ungodly coaches, when our daughters learn in modeling class how to be sultry and alluring, when our children learn in debating class how to demolish their opponents; they are "learning to imitate the detestable ways of the nations. You can't get from these things to living for the glory of God.

I am not saying that you cannot get from football or modeling or debate class to the glory of God. However, you cannot teach children to perform as non-Christians out of the values of non-Christians and expect them to see that life is about knowing and loving God. Ungodly mentors are already telling them that life is about something other than knowing God and living for His glory.

APPLICATION

It may be helpful for you to look at the issue of goals for your children through the lens of "what does it do for me?" Often parents are willing to run their kids from place to place and make incredible sacrifices because there is some payoff for them. They will gain the recognition. People will congratulate them when their children do well. Which items from this list of ungodly attitudes of heart might be motivating you to encourage the development of your children's skills?

- Anxiety
- Envy
- Love of self
- Covetousness
- Fear of man
- Pride
- Desire for approval
- Greed
- Selfish ambition

Romans 12:1–2 tells us not to allow the world to squeeze us into its mold.

Therefore, I urge you, brothers, in view of God's mercy, to offer your bodies as living sacrifices, holy and pleasing to God—this is your spiritual act of worship. Do not conform any longer to the pattern of this world, but be transformed by the renewing of your mind. Then you will be able to test and approve what God's will is—his good, pleasing and perfect will.

We all would like to do a better job of showing our children the excellence and greatness of God. 2 Thessalonians 1:10 says that in the day that Jesus Christ is revealed, we who have believed will marvel at Him. We will be caught up with the pleasurable experience of being dazzled and awed by the Lord of glory.

Psalm 145 speaks of the greatness of God that no one can fathom. Verse 4 of this Psalm describes parenting in terms of one generation telling the next generation of the splendor of the majesty of God and wonderful greatness of His works.

1. Make notes below on the excellence of God from Psalm 145.

_____

_____

_____

_____

_____

_____

It is against the backdrop of the greatness and soul satisfying goodness of God that we can seek to lure our children away from the fleeting pleasures of this earth to the soul fulfilling joys of knowing and serving God.

Some may be asking, "But what about my child's talents

and abilities?" The challenge before you is to think through this issue of developing your children's Godgiven abilities. Your task is to help them see their abilities as God given and themselves as stewards of the gifts of God. Matthew 25:14–30 provides us with good direction in thinking biblically about talents and abilities.

2. What principles regarding talents and abilities emerge from this parable?

_____

_____

_____

_____

_____

_____

Your task is to apply these principles to your instruction and leadership of your children.

STRATEGIC QUESTIONS

If you are going to help your children learn to live for the glory of God, you must hold before them at all times the fact that life is found in knowing God and living for His glory.

1. What are some of the ways you can do this?

_____

_____

_____

_____

2. Are there any activities that may not be wicked in themselves, but are turning your child's attention away from God and the supremacy of God?

_____

_____

_____

_____

3. What should you do to address these?

_____

_____

_____

_____

_____

4. What are some of the biblical nonnegotiables through which you must screen the activities of your children to insure that that are not in conflict with the goal of training them to live for the glory of God? You should be able to come up with five or six. I'll get you started:

The activity must not conflict with worship on the Lord's Day.

_____

_____

_____

_____

_____

As we have seen in some of the passages we have studied in this chapter, life that it truly life is found in knowing God. All true joys and delights are found in him. By faith we believe that joy, happiness, contentment, pleasure and satisfaction, both in this world and the world to come, are found in knowing and serving the living God. The most powerful way to teach that to your kids is to believe it and live it yourself.

CONCLUDING THOUGHTS

We have been confronted with searching and convicting truths. The promise of God is that He draws near to those who draw near to Him.

1. Find phrases in the passages below with which you can fortify yourself and encourage your heart as you show your kids the glories of God.

James 1:22–25 _____

_____

_____

James 4:7–10 _____

_____

_____

2 Peter 3:10–14 _____

_____

_____

2 Corinthians 6:14–7:1 _____

_____

_____

2. How can you pray for yourself and your friends in light of
    these passages of Scripture?

    _____

    _____

    _____

    _____

    _____

    _____

    _____

    _____

    _____

    _____

    _____

    _____

    _____

    _____

    _____

    _____

    _____

    _____

    _____

    _____

    _____

    _____

    _____

CHAPTER 5

Discarding
Unbiblical Methods

THE BIG IDEA

Perhaps you have not thought through the methodology of
your parenting; you just do it. You may be reflecting the parenting that was modeled for you, or you find things that you
hear on a television news magazine compelling. You may be
influenced by what friends say works for them. Whatever methods you employ probably have this in common. They are di-
rected toward behavior - curbing behavior you do not want
and encouraging behavior you think is good. Whether you
threaten, encourage, yell a lot, bribe, offer stickers or some
other rewards, the common objective is to modify behavior.
The problem is that since the heart and behavior are so closely
linked, whatever modifies behavior inevitably trains the heart.
When you appeal to the fear of man (what will others think
of you?) to get your children to perform, you train their hearts
to the fear of man. When you appeal to the love of pleasure,
you train their hearts to the love of pleasure. When you promise the trinkets and babbles they like, you train their hearts to
the love of possessions. Whatever constrains behavior trains
the heart. Methods, therefore, are important. The methods
you use must focus on shepherding the heart toward understanding how to live as one created by God, for God.

This chapter discusses the information in Chapter 7 of *Shepherding a Child's Heart.*

DIGGING INTO THE WORD

1. God is not simply concerned with the externals of behavior, God is concerned with the heart. How do these passages make this clear?

Proverbs 4:23 _____

_____

1 Samuel 16:7_____

_____

2 Chronicles 16:9_____

_____

Deuteronomy 10:12–13_____

_____

Ezekiel 14:1–8_____

_____

Joel 2:12–13 _____

_____

2. The Bible also has much to say about the relationship of behavior to the heart. Notice how these passages make that connection.

Matthew 5:28 _____

_____

Matthew 15:18_____

_____

Mark 7:21–23 _____

_____

3. To take this all one step further, the Bible also teaches that
    when the heart is cleansed, the behavior will take care of
    itself.

Matthew 23:26 _____

_____

Ezekiel 36:25–27_____

_____

No wonder David prays as he does in Psalms 51:10, 17:

> Create in me a pure heart, O God, and renew a steadfast
> spirit within me. . . The sacrifices of God are a broken spirit;
> a broken and contrite heart, O God, you will not despise.

APPLICATION

1. Here is a question that we must think about. What is the
    point of appeal in many of our child training methods?
    The first couple blanks have been filled in for you.

Training method	Point of appeal
Bribery	*Child's greed*
Shaming children	*Child's emotions*
Offering prizes	_____
Punishment	_____
Grounding	_____
Contracts	_____

Ignoring bad behavior   _____

Praising good behavior   _____

Time out   _____

Yelling and screaming   _____

I once thought the problem with these methods was that they did not shepherd the heart, but I came to realize that all we do shepherds the heart. These methods simply shepherd the heart in the wrong direction. They may train the heart to love money, to fear privation, to fear man, to desire approval, to demand rights, to live for rewards, naming just a few. The problem is not that they do not shepherd the heart; they shepherd it in the wrong direction. Behavior and the heart are joined in such a way that whatever constrains behavior, also trains the heart. Perhaps, like many people you can see the ways that many of the things you do not like about yourself are related to the ways the adults in your world constrained your behavior. Patterns of false guilt, fear of man, shame and so forth often reflect life experience.

One of the problems with unbiblical methods is that they are some form of behaviorism. The goal is changed behavior. The method is designed to produce a change from unacceptable to acceptable behavior. Effective behaviorism works. It is possible to employ behaviorism and modify the behavior of a child. An illusion is created that things are under control and the child is getting better. But if we peel back the layers and look at the heart issues, things are far more bleak. The child who is trained by behaviorism is learning a false basis for ethics. He is taught that the basis for right behavior is not the being and existence of God and his revelation (who the Lord is and what he has said). It is rather, "What will get me what I want or help me avoid what I don't want?" Either way (whether the point of appeal is negative or positive) the child is being taught a self-centered basis for ethics. No wonder Paul warns us against the influence of the culture.

2.   Think about these passages and how they apply to the discussion at hand.

> See to it that no one takes you captive through hollow and deceptive philosophy, which depends on human tradition and the basic principles of this world rather than on Christ.
>
> *Colossians 2:8*

_____

_____

_____

_____

_____

_____

_____

> Do not conform any longer to the pattern of this world, but be transformed by the renewing of your mind. Then you will be able to test and approve what God's will is—his good, pleasing and perfect will.   *Romans 12:2*

_____

_____

_____

_____

_____

_____

STRATEGIC QUESTIONS

You need to ask yourself some tough questions like the following:

- What am I expecting will motivate my child to hear my correction?
- What am I using in this discipline situation to encourage behavior that I think is appropriate?
- In this discipline situation, what is the point of appeal to my child?
- Am I speaking to the root issue or to the fruit issue?
- How will this correction, discipline or motivational statement move him to right behavior from right motives?

Remember, unbiblical methods that focus on constraining behavior in some manner will inevitable lead to superficiality in our parenting. Since they only address behavior they will miss the point of biblical discipline. When you are tempted to be an externalist like the Pharisees (Matthew 23:5), remember Jesus' words to the Pharisees in Matthew 23:26, "Blind Pharisee! First clean the inside of the cup and dish, and then the outside also will be clean."

For you to change your style of parenting and focus on root issues rather than fruit issues will require change in your ways of thinking. Identify some of those changes.

_____

_____

_____

_____

_____

_____

_____

CONCLUDING THOUGHTS

1. God is your ally as you seek to deal with root issues in your parenting. God is the searcher of hearts. Make notes on the ways this is expressed in the following passages.

Psalm 139:23–24 _____

_____

_____

Hebrews 4:12–13 _____

_____

_____

1 Chronicles 28:9 _____

_____

_____

Psalm 26:2 _____

_____

_____

While you are not the searcher of hearts and you must avoid assigning motivations to your children, you *can* pray that God, who does search hearts, will help you and your children to understand the things that push and pull their behavior.

The things you have been thinking about in this chapter place you squarely into spiritual warfare. It is not easy to deviate so radically from the norms and practices of the culture around you. You risk being misunderstood. You may sometimes feel lonely. You will have times of doubting whether you are on the right track.

2. The Word of God fortifies you for spiritual battle. Take time to read through Ephesians 6:10–18 and make notes of encouragement for yourself.

_____

_____

_____

_____

_____

_____

_____

_____

_____

_____

_____

_____

_____

_____

_____

_____

_____

CHAPTER 6

Embracing Biblical Methods—Communication

THE BIG IDEA

If asked whether you have good communication skills, you would probably think of your ability to express your ideas with words. But the finest art of communication is not the ability to express your ideas and thoughts; it is the ability to understand the thoughts of others. Good communication is not just the ability to explain and instruct; it is the ability to understand the other person and help them articulate the inner world of their thoughts and ideas. Each of us has had conversations in which we spoke with someone who understood us and made it easy for us to express our ideas. Have you not found such conversations delightful and savored them with joy? You need to know how to communicate with your children in ways that make it easy for them to express their ideas and thoughts. You have to get to the heart. Remember, they live out of their hearts.

This chapter discusses the information found in Chapter 8 of *Shepherding a Child's Heart*.

DIGGING INTO THE WORD

In this Bible study section, you will be presented with a series of passages. The questions about these passages are designed to lead your thinking to a dimension of communication that focuses on understanding others rather than merely expressing your own thoughts and ideas. There is a valid place for learning to express your ideas more fully. We will explore that in the next chapter.

> A fool finds no pleasure in understanding but delights in airing his own opinions. *Proverbs 18:2*

1. What is communication all about for this man who is called a fool?

   _____

   _____

   _____

2. What is it like to talk with someone who delights in understanding you? What kinds of activities would the person who delights in understanding undertake in conversation? Describe a conversation with a person who delights in understanding you.

   _____

   _____

   _____

   _____

   _____

   _____

3. What is it like to talk with someone whose only interest in conversation is airing his own ideas and thoughts (especially if you are being reproved by those ideas and thoughts)? Describe a conversation in which you are being corrected and rebuked, but the person speaking to you is not really interested in your reasoning and thoughts.

    _____

    _____

    _____

    _____

    _____

    _____

    _____

    _____

4. Why is the person whose focus of conversation is airing his own opinion, rather than delighting in understanding, considered a fool?

    _____

    _____

    _____

    _____

5. How many times have you been a fool in conversation? (No number is needed, its just something to think about.)

    He who answers before listening—that is his folly and his shame.   *Proverbs 18:13*

6. It seems so obvious that you should not answer before listening. What would prompt you (or me) to do that?

_____

_____

_____

_____

_____

_____

7. Why would Solomon call this shameful communication?

_____

_____

_____

_____

_____

8. What do you experience when someone responds to you before you have had the opportunity to fully express yourself?

_____

_____

_____

_____

_____

_____

It is interesting to note that the proverb before this one speaks of pride—"Before his downfall a man's heart is proud, but humility comes before honor" (v. 12)—and the one after it speaks of a crushed spirit—"A man's spirit sustains him in sickness, but a crushed spirit who can bear?" (v. 14). Could it be that pride is what causes a person to answer before listening and the result of doing so produces a crushed spirit?

There is another perspective from which we may look at this area of understanding the person with whom we are speaking. The writer of Hebrews makes quite a point of Jesus' identification with us in our humanity.

> Both the one who makes men holy and those who are made holy are of the same family. So Jesus is not ashamed to call them brothers . . . Since the children have flesh and blood, he too shared in their humanity . . . For this reason he had to be made like his brothers in every way, in order that he might become a merciful and faithful high priest in service to God, and that he might make atonement for the sins of the people. Because he himself suffered when he was tempted, he is able to help those who are being tempted.
>
> *Hebrews 2:11, 14, 17–18*

God, in redeeming, did not stand off in His heavens and merely speak to us words of reproof, correction and condemnation; he came and dwelled with us.

9. Locate phrases in the verses written above that describe Jesus' thorough identification with us.

_____

_____

_____

_____

_____

_____

_____

Here is the point. Jesus came to earth and lived in a body like yours. He experienced life in this world. He was sinned against. He faced the hostility of sinful men and women. He experienced the temptations that you experience (without sinning). He is able to enter into your world. He has looked at life through your eyes. And the writer even indicates that his capacity to help us when we are tempted is tied to his experience of temptation (Hebrews 2:18).

10. Some of the implications of Christ's incarnation and identification with us are worked out in Hebrews 4:14–16. What makes our great high priest able to sympathize with our weaknesses; what is the hope for you in your weakness?

_____

_____

_____

_____

_____

11. Notice in Hebrews 5:2 how the high priest is described. How does he deal with those who are ignorant and go astray?

_____

_____

_____

APPLICATION

1. If you are to make application of all this to your interaction with your children when they face temptation or weaknesses, or when they require correction and discipline, what are some models, principles and perspectives you can draw out of these passages in Hebrews 2, 4 and 5?

_____

_____

_____

_____

_____

_____

_____

2. As a godly parent you wish to get beyond the surface issues in the correction, discipline and motivation of your children. You have a genuine desire not just to reprove your children, but to understand them. What seems to get in the way of those desires when you are interacting with your children—especially if they have done something requiring correction, and direction?

_____

_____

_____

_____

_____

_____

_____

_____

_____

3. Look at Hebrews 4:12. It tells you that the Bible has been given to help you understand the things that lie beneath and motivate behavior—"the thoughts and attitudes of the heart." The Bible provides adequate descriptions of both the positive and the negative things that motivate behavior. Make a list of as many *biblical* terms as you can find that describe the "thoughts and attitudes of the heart." I will get you started.

Godly thoughts & attitudes	*Ungodly thoughts & attitudes*
Humility	Pride
Submission	Rebellion
Love	Hatred

_____

_____

_____

_____

_____

Ungodly thoughts and attitudes are not exclusive to your children. You, too, struggle with those things. When you are drawing the deep waters of motivations out of your children (Proverbs 20:5), you have the opportunity to identify with them. "Honey, Daddy, (Mommy) understands what you are struggling with (remember we do not have a high priest who is unable to sympathize with our weaknesses) and there is hope for people like you and Daddy. It is found in Jesus, who is full of grace and mercy (Hebrews 4:16).

You can sympathize with your child's temptation without excusing his sin. Isn't this what Jesus does?

STRATEGIC QUESTIONS

It is clear that if you are going to draw out the "deep waters" of the heart of your child, you must be looking at the "deep waters" of your heart as well.

1. Look back at your lists of godly and ungodly attitudes of heart from the application section above. Which of these are things concerning which you need to seek God for grace and help?

_____

_____

_____

_____

_____

_____

_____

_____

_____

_____

Your children are not self-conscious about the things that motivate them. Part of what you must do with your children is develop ways of encouraging them to think about what pushes and pulls behavior.

One way to do that is to provide formative correction. This is "before the event" correction. Think of formative correction as giving them ways of thinking that are biblical and true. Then in corrective discipline, "after the event" discipline, you can appeal to things they have already learned and thought about.

Take the time to discuss attitudes of heart with your children. Have them study the Bible with you and make little notebooks of terms and descriptions of attitudes of heart. Help them find biblical examples and illustrations. For example, look up all the verses you can find on pride and humility. Discuss what pride and humility look like in a child. This gives them some ways of understanding themselves and the things that push and pull their behavior.

2. Think about a typical correction or discipline situation that you often face. What are some questions that you can ask to draw out some of the things you have been talking

about in your formative correction times. Let me help you get started.

"Help me understand what you were thinking when..."

_____

_____

_____

_____

_____

_____

_____

_____

_____

_____

_____

CONCLUDING THOUGHTS

You have been confronted with some biblical ways of thinking about yourself and your children. You know that these things are true. People are heart driven. The Bible has been given to describe the thoughts and attitudes of the heart. The function of communication is not just expressing your ideas and thoughts, but understanding the person with whom you are talking. All these concepts are firmly rooted in God's revelation, the Bible.

1. Describe some ways that you wish to see your communication with your child change.

   _____

   _____

   _____

   _____

   _____

   _____

2. What are some ways that you need to seek God for internal change in order to change the ways you talk with your children?

   _____

   _____

   _____

   _____

   _____

   _____

3. What passages of Scripture can you find to encourage yourself with the hope of internal change—the kind of change needed for you to shepherd the hearts of your children?

   _____

   _____

   _____

   _____

4. Sometimes writing out a prayer of confession and commitment helps us to articulate our deepest longings for change and renewal. Express to God your prayers for better communication with your children.

_____

_____

_____

_____

_____

_____

_____

_____

_____

_____

_____

_____

_____

_____

_____

_____

_____

_____

CHAPTER 7

Embracing Biblical Methods—
Types of Communication

THE BIG IDEA

Parents can fall into "mono-speak" with their children. It will vary with each parent. One might yell most of the time. Another might plead a lot. Still another might order his/her children. Whatever the parenting style, parents tend to use the same type of communication all the time. The Word of God holds out something richer and more satisfying than that. The Scriptures direct us to provide differing nuances to conversation depending on the need of the child with whom we are speaking: "And we urge you, brothers, warn those who are idle, encourage the timid, help the weak, be patient with everyone" (1 Thessalonians 5:14). Idle children need a warning. Timid children need encouragement. Weak children need communication that helps. There are obvious problems if we fail to be sensitive to the needs of the child with whom we are speaking. It is a mistake to help the idle. Warning the timid may crush him. Just as God deals with each parent according to their needs, so parents must deal the with their children in a manner that suits the need of the moment.

This chapter discusses the information found in Chapter 9 of *Shepherding a Child's Heart*.

DIGGING INTO THE WORD

Chapter 9 of *Shepherding a Child's Heart* discusses eight different forms of communication that parents can use to enable their conversations with their children to address the needs of the moment. The list in chapter 9 is not exhaustive, but only suggestive of the differing forms of speaking that God has revealed in the Bible.

For each of the forms of communication discussed in chapter 9 there will be a passage or passages to study and questions to ask of the passage or passages.

Encouragement

Look at Romans 15:4–5. Ultimately God gives encouragement but he does so through means. The means is the Scripture.

1. What is the relationship between encouragement and the Scripture?

    _____

    _____

2. What does encouragement from the Scripture provide for your child?

    _____

    _____

Correction

Correction is like the carpenter's plumb line, it tells when things are out of alignment.

3. Look at the following passages to discern the benefits of heeding correction:

Proverbs 10:17	Proverbs 15:10
Proverbs 12:1	Proverbs 15:12
Proverbs 13:18	Proverbs 15:32
Proverbs 15:5	

4. Look at the same verses again and note what is true of the child who will not heed correction.

_____

_____

_____

_____

Again, the word of God is central in all these forms of communication—see 2 Timothy 3:15–17.

Rebuke

Study the following passages asking yourself the following questions:

Leviticus 19:17	Proverbs 15:31	Proverbs 27:5
Psalm 141:5	Proverbs 17:10	Ecclesiastes 7:5
Proverbs 3:11–12	Proverbs 19:25	Luke 17:3
Proverbs 13:1	Proverbs 25:12	Revelation 3:19

5. What are the blessings of a well placed rebuke?

_____

_____

_____

_____

6. What is the contrast between the way a foolish child and wise child responds to a rebuke?

_____

_____

_____

_____

7. How can you help your children have a biblical view of rebuke?

_____

_____

_____

Entreaty

Entreaty is earnest and intense conversation in which a parent bares his soul, urging and warning a child to walk in the paths of wisdom and faith. While this word is not used frequently in the Bible, examples of entreaty fill the book of Proverbs.

Note the following examples of entreaty.

Proverbs 1:8   Proverbs 27:9
Proverbs 4:10   Proverbs 23:15–26

8. Think of a list of issues where your children would receive benefit from timely, gracious, passionate and earnest entreaty.

_____

_____

_____

_____

_____

_____

Instruction

Search out the meat of these passages about instruction and ask the following questions of these passages:

Psalm 50:16–17	Proverbs 13:13
Proverbs 1:8	Proverbs 13:20
Proverbs 4:11	Proverbs 16:21, 23
Proverbs 8:10	Proverbs 19:20, 27
Proverbs 8:33	Ephesians 6:4

9. What becomes of children who reject biblical instruction?

_____

_____

_____

_____

10. What blessings crown the head of children who receive biblical instruction?

_____

_____

_____

_____

11. What things must a parent do to make instruction stick?
    How does one grease the wheels of instruction?

_____

_____

_____

_____

Warning

Warnings are communication that put children on notice concerning dangers. Children do not naturally enjoy warnings; they often regard them as unnecessarily negative and silly. Yet the Bible has a very thorough discussion of warnings. Studying the following passages, note some of the elements of the Bible's theology of warnings:

Psalm 19:11	Ezekiel 3:18–21
Psalm 81:8–9	Nehemiah 9:29–37
Ecclesiastes 4:13	Acts 20:31
Jeremiah 22:21	Hebrews 12:25

12. What are the blessings of responding to warnings?

_____

_____

_____

13. What happens when children do not respond faithfully?

_____

_____

14. What is the relationship between warnings and the sowing and reaping passages like Galatians 6:7–8?

_____

_____

_____

_____

15. Do a quick survey of Proverbs and note every passage which contains a warning. (The word warn or warning will not appear in the passage). I'll get you started.

Passage	Warning
Proverbs 1:10–19	
Proverbs 1:24–32	
Proverbs 2:18–19	

_____

_____

_____

_____

_____

_____

_____

_____

_____

_____

_____

_____

_____

_____

_____

_____

_____

_____

_____

_____

_____

_____

Teaching

Teaching is the process of imparting knowledge. In English the word is used as a verb to describe the activity of imparting knowledge and as a noun to describe the knowledge imparted. For us as Christian parents it is the essential task of transmitting to our children a worldview rooted in God's revelation.

16. Looking at the following passages, ask yourself questions about the content of teaching, the importance of teaching and the response to teaching:

Deuteronomy 6:1–2	Psalm 119	Proverbs 9:9–12
Psalm 34:11–16	Proverbs 1:8–9	Proverbs13:14
Psalm 78:1–4	Proverbs 3:1	Isaiah 48:17–19
Psalm 86:11	Proverbs 4:2–4	2 Timothy 3:16
Psalm 90:12	Proverbs 6:20, 23	

_____

_____

_____

_____

_____

_____

_____

_____

_____

_____

Prayer

Prayer is an important aspect of parent-child communication. When you pray your children learn what matters to you. They learn how you think, they learn about the place God has in your life, they learn the nature of Christian experience and what is ultimate. Many wonderful prayers in the Bible teach of the being and existence of God, God's plan and the call on his people.

17. Study the following prayers. Note themes and lessons.

     1 Kings 8:23–53   Nehemiah 9:5–37
     Daniel 9:4–19   John 17

_____

_____

_____

_____

_____

_____

_____

_____

_____

Some people question the validity of praying in front of someone so they can hear and learn. The reasoning goes that prayer is thus perverted and its focus on God is lost on account of concern for the other hearers. We must surely avoid praying insincerely in a manner that manipulates human hearers. On this question it is instructive to note John 11:41–42.

APPLICATION

Remember that whether you are involved in encouragement, correction, rebuke, entreaty, instruction, warning, teaching or prayer, the Word of God is the basis for all you have to say. The Apostle puts it like this in Colossians 3:16, "Let the Word of Christ dwell in you richly as you teach and admonish one another. . ." The Word of Christ dwelling in you richly is what gives you something worthwhile to say during times of communication. Remember the words of Romans 10, "Faith comes by hearing, and hearing by the Word of Christ."

1. Taking each of the types of communication that we have examined in this chapter, develop three typical situations when one or more of these would be appropriate. I'll get you started.

    Situation: Your wife asks you to go out at 8:00 p.m. for milk. She has a $10 bill, so you get the milk and return home leaving the change on the kitchen counter. Later she asks for the change and you discover it is missing. None of your children has seen it. Picking up clothes after the kids are in bed, your wife discovers the exact change in your 14 year old daughter's jeans.

    Communication: Think through how to approach this situation. What combination of the eight types of communication will you use?

Situation:

_____

_____

_____

_____

Communication:

_____

_____

_____

_____

Situation:

_____

_____

_____

_____

Communication:

_____

_____

_____

_____

Situation:

_____

_____

_____

_____

Communication:

_____

_____

_____

_____

STRATEGIC QUESTIONS

You want your communication with your children to be constructive. You want it to reflect Ephesians 4:29: "Do not let any unwholesome talk come out of your mouths, but only what is helpful for building others up according to their needs, that it may benefit those who listen."

1. Most of us tend to get stuck in one primary communication style. What is yours? (It may not be one we have studied).

    _____

    _____

2. The passages that we studied in the DIGGING INTO THE WORD section of this chapter implied some mannerisms and character qualities that "grease the wheels" of successful communication. How many can you find?

    _____

    _____

    _____

3. Biblical forms of communication require time. What are some specific lifestyle, recreational, vocational changes

that you can make in order to have the time needed for communicating with your children in the way discussed above?

_____

_____

_____

CONCLUDING THOUGHTS

The Apostle speaks in 2 Corinthians 2:11 of Satan and his desire to outwit us with his schemes. I believe that one of the wily schemes of the Devil, if he cannot get us to reject truth outright, is to discourage us with ever being able to do what God has called us to. The scheme is to get us to look at our ordinary resources and then at the insurmountable nature of what God has called us to and to conclude, "There's no way. Not in this life. This is not possible."

If we come to these conclusions, we will run from the field of battle like the Israelites did in 1 Samuel 17. For 40 days, Goliath came out and taunted them. They looked at Goliath and concluded "There's no way. Not in this life. This is not possible." They looked at Goliath through the lens of their own strength and concluded they didn't have a chance.

David arrived and had hope for victory where they had been hopeless. You see, he had a different lens through which he looked at the situation. He looked at Goliath, he registered the fact that Goliath was 9 feet tall, but he drew a different conclusion. Seen through the lens of the greater size and power of God, David said, "Who is this uncircumcised Philistine that he should defy the armies of the living God?" Seen through the lens of the living God, the Philistine was reduced in size.

As you talk with your children, you are doing the work of

the living God. You are not up for the task. But nothing is too big for Him.

Write out a statement of commitment to God, to trust in His strength and to speak to your children in ways that are helpful, according to their needs, that they might benefit.

_____

_____

_____

_____

_____

_____

_____

_____

_____

_____

_____

_____

_____

_____

_____

_____

_____

CHAPTER 8

Embracing Biblical Methods—
A Life of Communication

THE BIG IDEA

Communication is essential to the nature of Christian faith. When God created Adam and Eve the first thing he did was speak to them. Even in Paradise they needed communication. They needed for God to tell them who they were and what they were to do. We serve a God who reveals Himself to people, not only in concrete ways in his creation, but who gives them truth - truth written down in a fixed form. He has revealed an entire book. Communication and truth are important to God. Thus, communication is essential for us as we shepherd our children. Communication is a primary means of discipling our children. It is a primary means by which we shepherd their hearts. Many passages in Scripture show the primacy and power of rich, thorough communication with our children. Shepherding the hearts of your children requires a lifestyle of communication.

This chapter discusses the information found in Chapter 10 of *Shepherding a Child's Heart.*

DIGGING INTO THE WORD

Communication is essential if children are to walk in the ways of God. Below are some passages that demonstrate the Bible's vision for our communication with our children.

1. *Read Deuteronomy 6.* Note the following:

    • The goal of this communication is three generations who live in the fear of the Lord and obey his commands (Deuteronomy 6:2–3).
    • The primary means to reach this goal is passionate communication—talking about God all the time (Deuteronomy 6:7).
    • Communication about truth is so essential that even their clothing and household decorations are to convey truth (Deuteronomy 6:8–9).
    • Consistent lifestyle choices to follow the ways of God and be different than the nations around them will provide the context for future conversation with the children. It is in the context of being different from the other nations that the questions and answers of truth come up (Deuteronomy 6:13–25).
    • The father speaks from deep spiritual connection with truth, not from a mere theoretical knowledge of abstract ideas (Deuteronomy 6:4–6).

2. *Read Psalm 145.* The parenting task is described in verse 4: "One generation will commend your works to another; they will tell of your mighty acts."

    If one generation will devote itself to commending God's works, to telling of his mighty acts, they must themselves be overwhelmed with the glory and grandeur of God. (Psalm 145:1–3). You cannot give away what you don't have.

Note the specific content of the declaration of God's glory. It is His own being, "the glorious splendor of [his] majesty" (verse 5). It is what he does, "his wonderful and awesome works and great deeds" (verses 5–6).

The remainder of the Psalm is descriptive of God's being and his works. Verse 21 is a response of any sober person who is dazzled by God's glory: "My mouth will speak in praise of the LORD. Let every creature praise his holy name for ever and ever."

3. *Glance through the book of Proverbs.* Every "Listen, my son . . ." or "Pay attention, my son . . ." section of Proverbs illustrates the call to a lifestyle of communication.

Notice with me that in all three of these examples the content of communication is not just nice, innocuous conversation. The communication has the content of God's glory and greatness, his mighty acts of power and his rich and grand acts of redemption.

APPLICATION

Communication rooted in God's glory and goodness, his mighty acts and his grand redemption requires a mom or dad who is overwhelmed by the soul satisfying goodness of God. You, as the parent, must be a person who understands both your own fallen nature and the work that Christ has done to provide forgiveness of sin and empowerment for living. So our message is not, "be like me," but rather, "come with me to where sinners find forgiveness and grace".

In a section on page 98 of *Shepherding a Child's Heart*, we read, "[I]nfluence represents the willingness of a child to place himself under authority because of trust. This trust has several elements. Children trust you when they know you love them and are committed to their good, when they know you understand them, when they know you understand their strengths and their weaknesses, when they know you have invested yourself in encouragement, correction, rebuke, entreaty, instruction, warning, teaching and prayer. When a child knows that all his life you have sought to see the world through his eyes, he will trust you. When he knows that you have not tried to make him like you or like anybody else, but only sought to help him realize his full potential as a creature God made to know Him and live in the relationship of fellowship with Him, he will trust you."

1. Evaluate the things that must be in place for this to describe your relationship with your children. Include the full range of Christian life issues—from your personal walk with God to lifestyle, work, and values issues.

2. Plan some contexts for conversations like the ones described in the three passages above. You might want to think in terms of formal and informal conversations.

Formal conversations: Family worship; one-on-one Bible studies with you kids

Others:_____

_____

_____

_____

_____

Informal conversations: Next time you are in the van together; Taking your child to breakfast

Others:_____

_____

_____

_____

_____

STRATEGIC QUESTIONS

1. Part of the sharing that we do in communication is not just truths about God (as important as that is) or assessment of our children's conduct or development (as necessary as that is), but also the dynamics of the Christian life.

   As with everything else this must be done using the Word of God, not just our words. What passages would you turn to with your child to discuss the following:

Sonship with the Father:_____

Repenting of your sins:_____

Finding comfort from God: _____

Thankfulness for mercies:_____

Finding forgiveness from God and man:_____

Strength in temptation: _____

Joy in trials: _____

Joy in serving others:_____

Hope of glory: _____

Delights of knowing God: _____

2. People are convinced of the value of something before
    they will sacrifice to do it. The communication we have
    been studying will clearly require sacrifice. Let's think
    through the benefits.

How do your children benefit?_____

_____

_____

How do you benefit?_____

_____

_____

How is God glorified? _____

_____

_____

_____

CONCLUDING THOUGHTS

We live in a time and place in history when there is much to compete with time consuming communication. We have the capacity to go places and do things that have been unimaginable for most of human history. In addition, a whole virtual world is opening up on us and stealing away ever increasing chunks of our interest, energy and stamina.

Additionally, in our culture parenting has been reduced to child-care. So business and governmental leaders use the terms child-care and parenting interchangeably. The notion of parents being defined by the type of nurturing role that Deuteronomy 6 describes almost seems like a report from a planet long ago in a galaxy far away.

If we are going to do the things God calls us to do we must think in new ways. Romans 12:1–2 speaks to these issues with poignancy:

> Therefore, I urge you, brothers, in view of God's mercy, to offer your bodies as living sacrifices, holy and pleasing to God—this is your spiritual act of worship. *Do not conform any longer to the pattern of this world, but be transformed by the renewing of your mind.* Then you will be able to test and approve what God's will is—his good, pleasing and perfect will (emphasis added).

I write these things knowing that some readers will read them and think that I have overemphasized things in a manner that is not really practical. Some may be tempted to say, "Parents might have been able to do this stuff in Moses' day, but we live in different times." What is being suggested here is not impossible, it's just not according to the pattern of this world.

If your desire is to not raise Christian cynics who have a "form of godliness, but deny its power" (2 Timothy 3:5), then you must turn from the temptation to respond to these chapters on communication in a cynical manner.

What commitments are you prepared to make in order to have the kind of communication we have discussed in these last three chapters?

_____

_____

_____

_____

_____

_____

Psalm 29 is a favorite Psalm. In short, crisp, powerful phrases it describes God's awesome power. His voice breaks the cedars, it strikes with flashes of lightening, it shakes the desert and strips the forest bare and all in his temple cry, "GLORY!" The Psalmist ends with two powerful conclusions: *The LORD gives strength to his people; the LORD blesses his people with peace.*

The two things you need, strength and peace, are given by God. Go to him for the strength and serenity you need to do what God calls you to and then sit down and talk to your kids about it.

CHAPTER 9

Embracing Biblical Methods—The Rod

THE BIG IDEA

While we are living during an era when the idea of spanking children is not popular, it is something God has called us to do. Children are not born ethically and morally neutral. Their needs are more profound than the obvious needs for instruction and correction. The child's need is not an information deficit; his problem is his heart. He has a heart that has strayed from God's ways like a lost sheep. There are things going on within that are ugly and if allowed to bloom and grow and bear fruit they will bring his life to destruction. The folly that is in his heart must be driven out. God says that the rod of correction is the means by which this happens. *Folly is bound up in the heart of a child, but the rod of discipline will drive it far from him (Proverbs 22:15).* God tells us that the rod of correction is what our children need. He has not revealed how it all works. Therefore, the faithful use of the rod is not based on our ability to rationalize how and why it works; it is rather based on faith in what God has said. For parents, the use of the rod is a question of whether we will trust and obey God.

This chapter discusses the information found in Chapter 11 of *Shepherding a Child's Heart.*

DIGGING INTO THE WORD

As we look to the Bible we see two things that underscore the importance of the faithful use of the rod of correction. First, the problem of sin in the child that places the child on a path of destruction—both temporally and ultimately. Second, the command to use the rod of discipline as a means of turning the child out of the path of destruction.

Folly is Bound Up in the Heart of A Child

As hard as it is to face when you see the delightful smiles of youngsters whom you love, your children are sinners. The Bible does not say that they are as bad as they could be, it simply recognizes that the fundamental problem of humanity is not external, but internal. It is not the effect of the environment on the child; it is the child. Your children are sinners.

1. Using the passages below, write out the words that describe the problem of sin in your children.

Romans 3:10–18 _____

_____

_____

Titus 3:3 _____

_____

Ephesians 2:1–3 _____

_____

_____

   Lest we think this is an adult problem the Bible makes it clear that the fallen state of humanity is a child problem too.

Psalm 51:5 _____

_____

Psalm 58:3 _____

_____

Proverbs 22:15 _____

_____

The reason our children require the rod of correction is that they have an internal problem. They have strayed from the ways of God like lost sheep. They are filled with a compulsive selfishness and self-interest that will bring both temporal and eternal destruction on their heads. The rod of correction is given for this purpose.

The Rod of Correction Will Drive It Far From Him

We do not employ the rod of correction because *we* looked at our child and decided, "What this child needs is a good spanking." We use the rod of correction because *God* reveals truth to parents and says, "What your child needs is a good spanking." The rod of correction is a response of obedience and faith on the part of a parent. The parent is trusting in God who has said that the rod of correction will be the means through which children will escape the folly that is bound up in their hearts.

2. Look at the passages below and note phrases that command the use of the rod.

Proverbs 13:24 _____

_____

Proverbs 22:15 _____

_____

Proverbs 23:13–14 _____

_____

Proverbs 29:15 _____

_____

Why has the rod of correction fallen into disuse in our time? It is not that the passages above are unclear or obscure. They are not difficult to understand and interpret. The problem is that the rod is out of style in our day. It is not fashionable. We are influenced by non-biblical critiques of the rod and by the more popular ideas about discipline that our culture provides.

Our problem is the problem warned against in Colossians 2:8:

> See to it that no one takes you captive through hollow and deceptive philosophy, which depends on human tradition and the basic principles of this world rather than on Christ.

Q   When are captives taken?

A   During a war. There is a war going on for our families and captives are being taken. The integrity and wisdom of our Commander is under question. Parents are being taken captive to non-biblical thinking about child rearing.

Q   How are captives being taken?

A   Through hollow and deceptive philosophies. Note those words, "hollow and deceptive." These philosophies look substantial. They sound solid and stable. They seem persuasive on the evening news and other unimpeachable sources of wisdom and goodness. But they are hollow and deceptive.

Q On what are these hollow and deceptive philosophies based?

A They are based on human traditions and the ways of the world. They are rooted in whatever is the prevailing notion of the day - the fashionable concepts in the traditions of the marketplace of ideas.

Q On what are they not based?

A These hollow and deceptive philosophies are not based on Christ and his revelation.

The Bible is not unclear about the rod of correction. The words are easy to understand. Will you be will be more influenced by the fashionable ideas of the culture or the clear teaching of the Bible?

APPLICATION

As we use the rod of correction, we must make a distinction between behavior that is childish and behavior that is defiant. Young children do many childish things. They are clumsy. They don't think through the implications of their silliness. Many things that children do that are inconvenient are not defiant. The rod is for defiant behavior not for childish or even inconvenient behavior.

1. Think of illustrations of the difference between behavior that is childish and behavior that is defiant.

_____

_____

_____

_____

_____

_____

_____

2. Many wrong ideas about discipline are addressed in the
   Hebrews 12 passage that speaks of God's discipline of us
   and parallels it with the parent's discipline of their child.
   Make a study of Hebrews 12:5–11, asking the following
   questions of the text.

   a. What phrases show that discipline is an expression of
      love?

   _____

   _____

   _____

   b. What does failure to discipline on the part of a father
      signal?

   _____

   _____

   _____

   c. What phrases show the purpose of discipline to be pos-
      itive rather than punitive?

   _____

   _____

   _____

d. What are some of the results of discipline?

_____

_____

_____

e. What phrases show that we should not expect the process to be fun?

_____

_____

_____

f. What does discipline produce in the parent-child relationship?

_____

_____

_____

g. Other observations?

_____

_____

_____

STRATEGIC QUESTIONS

1. Why is it so difficult to spank your children consistently? Why are you so often tempted to let things go?

_____

_____

_____

_____

_____

2. What promises and perspectives from the Scripture passages cited in this chapter can give you impetus and encouragement to be faithful and timely in discipline?

_____

_____

_____

3. Most parents have experienced times when they have come to their children in discipline with a sinful anger that left them defeated and their child wounded. Look at the following passages, noting the contrast between interactions driven by the energy of sinful anger and godly interaction that is fueled by imitation of Christ.

Ephesians 4:31–32 _____

_____

_____

_____

Colossians 3:8–12 _____

_____

_____

_____

Comment on James 1:19–20 _____

_____

_____

_____

It is clear from these passages that we cannot come to our kids in correction and discipline with our teeth bared and full of rage and anger. The energy behind our discipline must be love for God and love for our children. Our motive in discipline should be restoration, not retribution. None of this emphasis is a denial that it is possible to experience righteous anger that is not sinful and wicked (see 1 Corinthians 13:5, James 1:19, Ephesians 4:26). Perhaps this distinction would be helpful. Righteous anger (like Jesus displays in the Temple in John 2) is because God is dishonored, not because of personal affront or inconvenience.

4. What are the problems in you that make you susceptible to the temptation to discipline in anger?

_____

_____

_____

_____

5. What changes can you make in your approach to discipline and correction that will help you not muddy the waters with anger?

_____

_____

_____

_____

_____

If you are a person who struggles with sinful anger, and are often tempted (and sometimes succumb) to fly at your kids in a rage, you must take some positive steps to protect yourself and your children from abusing correction and discipline.

Will you make the following pledge to your spouse and your children?

> I will never undertake any physical discipline of the children, until I have first gotten alone with God to quiet my heart before Him. Only when my heart is right will I follow through with the appropriate discipline.

CONCLUDING THOUGHTS

The exhortations to turn away from anger that we saw above in Ephesians 4 and Colossians 3 are embedded in God's redemption.

The exhortations of Ephesians 4:25–32 find their power in the grace of God described in Ephesians 4:20–24:

> You, however, did not come to know Christ that way. Surely you heard of him and were taught in him in accordance with the truth that is in Jesus. You were taught, with regard to your former way of life, to put off your old self, which is being corrupted by its deceitful desires; to be made new in the attitude of your minds; and to put on the new self, created to be like God in true righteousness and holiness.

In the same way the "put off" and "put on" instructions of Colossians 3:5–17 are enabled by the grace of redemption described in Colossians 3:1–4:

> Since, then, you have been raised with Christ, set your hearts on things above, where Christ is seated at the right hand of

God. Set your minds on things above, not on earthly things. For you died, and your life is now hidden with Christ in God. When Christ, who is your life, appears, then you also will appear with him in glory.

The exhortations to put off anger and put on gentleness and compassion, or to follow through consistently with discipline when you dread the confrontation, find their strength not in your determinations to do better, but in the redemptive power of God that is your Savior, Jesus Christ.

Augustine said it well 1600 years ago. "Lord, give what you command and then command what you will."

CHAPTER 10

Embracing Biblical Methods—
Appeal to the Conscience

THE BIG IDEA

Two concerns dominate this chapter. The first is the concern to keep your discipline and correction focussed on the conscience of your children. The second is the importance of keeping the centrality of the cross and the redemptive work of Christ as the goal of all your nurturing. Instruction, motivation, discipline and correction will misfire if the gospel is not central and the conscience is not the target. The wrong focus is your offenses, hurts, unhappiness, desires, dreams, hopes and fears. The right focus is the gospel of grace and your children's need to know and love and serve God. The wrong focus leads to endless debate and argument. Keeping the focus on biblical truth and appealing to the conscience leaves your child's controversy with God and not with you. Whenever long discussions can take place without opening the Bible or talking about repentance, forgiveness and enablement from Christ, you have gotten off track.

This chapter discusses the information found in Chapter 12 of *Shepherding a Child's Heart*.

DIGGING INTO THE WORD

The Bible speaks in many places about the conscience. I am persuaded that we have not thought enough about the Bible's teaching about the conscience and appealing to the conscience in motivation, discipline and correction. Let's do a brief study on the conscience.

1. Look up Romans 2:14–15 and answer the following questions:

    a. What phrases describe the activities of the conscience?

    _____

    _____

    b. What proof do you have that the conscience works even if people are not believers?

    _____

    _____

2. Look up 2 Corinthians 4:1–6 and answer the following questions:

    a. What arc the negative and positive statements of verse 2 that describe how we commend ourselves to the conscience?

    _____

    _____

    _____

    _____

    _____

b. What would be examples of secret and shameful ways that are deceptive and distort the truth that are sometimes used by parents in the place of commending themselves to the conscience?

_____

_____

_____

_____

_____

_____

c. What do you think are some of the blinders that the god of this age uses (verse 4) to keep your children from seeing the glory of Christ?

_____

_____

_____

_____

_____

_____

d. Describe the focal point of the message according to verse 5.

_____

_____

_____

_____

e. According to verse 6 what hope do you have as you faithfully proclaim the glories of Christ and the demands of truth to your children?

_____

_____

_____

_____

4. Look at Titus 1:14–16 and 1 Timothy 4:1–2. These passages describe a possibility that should strike terror into the heart of any serious person. Note the two phrases used to describe a malfunctioning conscience.

_____

_____

_____

_____

_____

5. This should not leave you hopeless—God's grace is powerful—but it should alert you to true danger. Think of how you could talk to your children about this danger. Script the outline of the conversation.

_____

_____

_____

_____

_____

_____

6. Hebrews 9:14 and Hebrews 10:19–22 hold out real hope
    for the guilty conscience. Prepare yourself for conversa-
    tions in which you hold out this hope for your kids.

_____

_____

_____

_____

_____

Note how these passages all contain both focus points of
this chapter. Both the conscience and the redemptive work
of Christ are in view.

APPLICATION

If you are going to appeal to the conscience of your children,
you must use God's words and not your words. Let me give
you some examples. I'll do the first one and you can work on
the last two.

Example

You have had a conversation with your son over his failure to
take out the trash. Instead of receiving the reproof in humility, he is obviously miffed. His responses to you are sullen,
angry and generally disrespectful. At an appropriate time, you
could approach him and say something like, "Hey, John, I
want to discuss a passage of Scripture with you to help you with
something I think is really important for you." Have him look
at Proverbs 9:7–9. Then get him to fill in Figure 1 below.

Here are the questions that will enable him to fill in the
blanks.

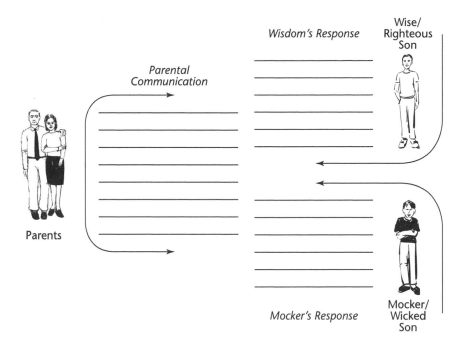

Figure 1 Responses to Parental Instruction

- There is a parent in this passage. What four words describe what the parent does? Is it wrong for the parent to do these things?
- There are two different responders to the parent and two names for each. What are they?
- How does the mocker/wicked man respond?
- How does the wise/righteous man respond?
- Which way of responding do you think you reflect most of the time? (No one is always, without exception, one place or the other.)
- Which describes how you are responding right now?
- What do you think describes what I long to see in you?
- What is God calling you to do in response to my parenting?

1. Your kids are watching something on TV that you do not think they should be watching. Obviously, you can go into the room and require them to shut it off, but you want something deeper than that. In addition to having the program shut off, you want them to be understanding, and living out of a sensitivity to the ways of God.

    a. Think through how Ephesians 5:1–11 speaks to these issues. Prepare to walk them through a critique of TV rooted in the revelation of God. What questions do you want to help them ask of the passage?

    _____

    _____

    _____

    _____

    _____

    _____

    _____

    _____

    b. How can you use this passage to appeal to the conscience?

    _____

    _____

    _____

    _____

    _____

2. Your teenage daughter is speaking to her younger sisters in ways that range between being unkind to them and denigrating them. You have spoken with her about it, but she thinks you are really going overboard. "This is just the way kids talk these days."

   Think through James 3 and prepare to talk to her about her ways of communicating. Outline how to walk her through the passage. Note especially verses 13–17. Help her critique whether her conversation reflects wisdom from above or from below. Keep the focus not on your thoughts and ideas, but on the Word of God. It is what God has said that she must contend with.

_____

_____

_____

_____

_____

_____

_____

_____

_____

_____

_____

_____

_____

_____

STRATEGIC QUESTIONS

1. What are some issues of the Christian life and growth in grace that must be in place for you to have the conversations we have outlined above with your kids? What fruit of the Spirit, what knowledge of truth must be in place if you are going to shepherd the hearts of your children?

_____

_____

_____

_____

_____

_____

_____

_____

2. Imagine having a conversation with your child in which you have been able to show him how much he has strayed from the ways of God and how much he needs not just to do better in the future, but how profoundly he needs the internal change that God gives through the gospel. What passages of Scripture could you take him to? What passages could fill him with hope of forgiveness and lasting change?

_____

_____

_____

_____

_____

_____

_____

_____

_____

_____

3. Make a list for yourself of ways that your parenting style must change if appeal to the conscience and the centrality of the person and work of Christ are to be your focus in the future.

   a. I must stop the following:

   _____

   _____

   _____

   _____

   _____

   b. In the future, by God's grace, I must:

   _____

   _____

   _____

   _____

   _____

Give yourself some practice. If you are studying this book with a group, practice role plays. Takes turns being the parents and think through how to engage the conscience.

CONCLUDING THOUGHTS

The key to all the fruitful ways that we want to deal with our children is doing the same things with ourselves. If we have well-worn paths to the cross where we find mercy and grace to help in our time of need, then we can help our children. Make a study of John 15:1–8, then answer the following questions.

1. What is the key to fruitfulness?

_____

_____

_____

2. How essential is it to remain in the vine?

_____

_____

_____

3. What are some of the disciplines of the Christian life that are essential to abiding/remaining in Christ?

_____

_____

_____

_____

4. Comment on John 15:5 in light of Philippians 4:13.

_____

_____

_____

_____

   You can learn to do this parenting task in new ways. You can learn to nurture your children. You can fill them with hope that is found in Christ, not in getting their act together. You can get beyond simply disapproving and condemning to deep conviction of sin through the work of God through his Word. The promise of this passage is that you can bear much fruit. This fruitfulness is found as you abide in Christ. It is found in what the older writers called "union and communion" with Christ.

5. What commitments of your own should you make for the glory of God and the good of your kids?

_____

_____

_____

_____

_____

_____

_____

_____

CHAPTER 11

Infancy to Childhood—
Goals and Methods

THE BIG IDEA

In the first five years the primary training objective is to teach your children to be people under authority. God—who is good, kind, gracious, and who has created us for his own glory; who provides everything for us to enjoy; in whom we live and move and have our being—has established authority structures and we are blessed as we live in submission to what God has ordained. The place of blessing for your child is found in obedience to you. This is what is good for him because it is what God has ordained. Teaching your child to be a person under authority is the goal. Faithful, timely use of the rod of correction coupled with gracious communication is the method. God has given us a goal for these early years and he has given us a means of working toward the goal. In this section we make application of the teaching on the rod found in chapter 9 of *Shepherding a Child's Heart*.

This chapter discusses the information found in Chapters 14 & 15 of *Shepherding a Child's Heart*.

DIGGING INTO THE WORD

The principle of obedience is greater than just a parent establishing his authority—it is teaching children how God has structured his world. There are authority structures in the world that God has established. It is the creature's calling to live under those authority structures; that is what it means to submit to God's authority. In the following passages identify the authority structures that God has established.

Romans 13:1–7 _____

_____

Ephesians 5:22–33_____

_____

Ephesians 6:1–3 _____

_____

Colossians 3:20 _____

_____

Titus 2:9–10_____

_____

Hebrews 13:17_____

_____

1 Peter 2:13–17 _____

_____

1 Peter 2:18–23 _____

_____

Children, as a result of the fall, have a natural resistance to authority. The problem children have with authority is exacerbated in our day by the fact that adults in general are not living under the authority structures that God has ordained for them. We often are not modeling for children the concept of entrusting oneself to God and living under the authorities God has ordained.

The real lesson for children and for adults is not that "father knows best." Father may, in fact, make mistakes. What a child may have confidence in is not father knowing best, but that God will protect and care for him as he submits to what God has ordained. This is a lesson that, sadly, is not being modeled for most children by the adults in their world.

So when we teach our children to obey us, the issue is not just that we wish to be obeyed and we are big enough to force them to do it; the issue is learning to live under the authority structures God has ordained.

This truth places everyday obedience in a larger context for our children. We teach them to obey and insist on their obedience and respect because it is what is good for them. They are learning to live in God's world under his authority with the confidence that God will bless them as they do so.

In a true sense even the issue of spanking our children is an issue of submitting to authority. God, who is wise and good in all his ways, has called me as a parent to the task of discipline. He says that I should spank my children.

The issue is not:

- Do I think this is a good way to teach children?
- Do I understand how it works?
- Was I ever physically abused as a child?
- Will my in-laws approve?
- Is it a popular idea about child rearing?
- What's wrong with time out?
- In the 21st century can't we think of a better way?

- Won't they grow up to hate me?
- Will it confuse them and make them hitters?

The issue is:

- Has God called me to spank my children? [On that question see Proverbs 13:24, 22:15, 23:13–14, 29:15,17]
- Will I trust and obey God?
- Will I live under God's authority or my own?

APPLICATION

In our culture parents are often unsure about their authority. We don't like authority. We don't like being the heavy. We want our children to do the right thing without being told. We surrender too many issues to the child's choice, especially with young children.

Let's revisit the illustrations in chapter 3. Parents give away their authority—they do it like this:

> I'm sorry, honey, mommy forgot that you don't like oatmeal. Now let's see, would you like sugar pops or toaster tarts?

Instead, Mom should say,

> Honey, we are having oatmeal today, it is good nutritious food, so we are going to pray and thank God for it and eat it with a cheerful heart. Maybe another day we will have something you like better, but today we are having oatmeal.

Here's another example:

> Honey, do you want to play T-ball or not? If you want to play T-ball you have to go to the practice. If you don't want to play just tell Daddy. You can do whatever you want.

Instead, Dad should say,

> Honey, your mother and I think it would be good for you to play T-ball. So this is what we are going to do.

Or,

> We don't think it would be good for you or for our family, so we aren't going to do it this year. Perhaps another year.

Here's a conversation we've all either had or overheard:

PARENT: Darling, you can't wear that party dress and those patent leather shoes today—we are going on a picnic and I want you to have fun.

CHILD: [Whining, demanding tone] But, I want to wear them. Jennifer hasn't seen them yet.

PARENT: But, Darling, they will get spoiled—please change into some jeans.

CHILD: [Negotiating tone] Mommy, I'll be careful, I'll just sit at the picnic table.

PARENT: OK, dear, I don't think it is good idea, and if your dress gets ruined, don't come crying to me.

Mother walks away thinking she is teaching this 5 year old to be a decision-maker.

The best way to teach children to be decision-makers is to model for them good decision-making. Make decisions for yourself and for them that reflect biblical principles. Take them into your confidence; tell them why you have made the decisions you have made, but be willing to be the authority in their lives. They need an authority that is kind—a benevolent despot in their lives.

Another question about authority and discipline concerns when to spank young children. Especially in the early years, when teaching children to be people under authority is the issue, we must discipline for issues of defiance rather than simply issues of behavior.

For example, I am not concerned about whether the two year old remembers not to throw his food from the high chair. I am willing to remind him every day not to throw his food. The real concern is defiant behavior. When I have told him not to throw his food and he looks me in the eye and throws the food as if to say, "There, I did it, and what are you going to do about it?"—that is defiant behavior.

I am willing to remind a toddler not to take the leaves off the houseplants. But when I remind him and he starts pulling off leaves, then I am dealing with defiance.

I am willing to clean up the spills made because clumsy little hands slipped with the glass of orange juice. I am willing to deal with the inconveniences of childishness and childish behavior.

I want to discipline the failure to honor and failure to obey. In terms of chapter 15 of *Shepherding a Child's Heart,* I want to discipline my child for leaving the circle, not for being a child.

In spanking, presentation is important. The message is not, "I've had it with you and you are going to get it now." When we come to our children in anger with our teeth bared, we are planting seeds of rebellion that will sprout and grow later.

The message is, "Honey, I love you and you have not obeyed Mommy. God says you must obey, so Mommy can't just let this go. You haven't obeyed, so Mommy is going to have to discipline you. You have moved outside the circle where God says it will go well for you and you will enjoy long life. I love you too much to say it doesn't matter, so Mommy is going to spank you."

It should *never* be, "I've had it with you"—rather, it should always be, "I am committed to you and to your good, so I am willing to do what is hard to do out of love for you."

STRATEGIC QUESTIONS

1. In what areas, if any, have you made your preschool children decision-makers rather than teaching them to be under authority?

_____

_____

_____

_____

_____

2. Perhaps even more subtly, what are the ways in which you communicate the idea that your child has to agree with you in order to obey?

_____

_____

_____

_____

_____

3. What are the situational pressures that you must avoid if you are to keep a clear focus on this task of teaching your children to be under authority?

_____

_____

_____

_____

_____

4. Think about your child and ask yourself the question, "What are the typical 'authority struggles' that I have with this child?"

_____

_____

_____

_____

_____

5. Develop a plan to graciously and firmly confront these "authority struggles" using clear communication of God's call to be a person under authority, and the gracious, measured use of the rod of correction. Think through the words you want to say and how to administer the rod.

_____

_____

_____

_____

6. What are some of the "abundance of the heart" issues for you that keep you from being gracious, kind, self-controlled and focussed on biblical goals as you teach your children to be people under authority and administer discipline?

_____

_____

_____

_____

7. Perhaps you have children who are 6, 8, 10, or 12 and they do not understand the concept of being a person under authority. How can you teach them these things in ways that are gracious and kind? Prepare some thoughts you could sit down and teach to your children so they can understand these important concepts.

_____

_____

_____

_____

_____

_____

CONCLUDING THOUGHTS

Many of us are nearsighted. Rather than working with a long-term vision, we settle for surviving the day. In fact, much of our living gets done in survival mode. Many years ago a godly man taught me that I needed to have a three generation vision. I needed to be concerned with my walk with God, my children's walk, and their children's walk. I remember his words as he talked with me about Deuteronomy 6, "You must be raising your children with a concern for where your grandchildren will be 50 years from now." It seemed light years away at the time, but now I have grandchildren and in 20 years those 50 years will be upon me.

Deuteronomy gives us this three generation vision. We train our children "[S]o that you, your children and their children after them may fear the LORD your God as long as you live by keeping all his decrees and commands that I give you, and so that you may enjoy long life" (Deuteronomy 6:2). There it is, three generations, "you, your children, their children."

How can we do this? It seems to be such a big task. We often find ourselves overwhelmed. Deuteronomy 6 gives us some help.

> Love the LORD your God with all your heart and with all your soul and with all your strength. These commandments that I give you today are to be upon your hearts. Impress them on your children. Talk about them when you sit at home and when you walk along the road, when you lie down and when you get up. *Deuteronomy 6:5–7*

Deuteronomy 6:5—*Love the LORD your God with all your heart and with all your soul and with all your strength.* It is out of wholehearted love for God that we shepherd our children. Loving God, delighting in Him and drawing near to Him, enables and empowers our diligent pursuit of these shepherding goals. It all starts with our love for God.

Deuteronomy 6:6—*These commandments that I give you today are to be upon your hearts.* As these things fill our hearts they overflow naturally into all of life. The goodness of obedience to God must fill our hearts. The wisdom of walking in God's truth must be on our hearts. The joy of life with God, even in the face of things that are hard and that we don't like, must fill our hearts. We cannot give away what we don't have.

Deuteronomy 6:7—*Impress them on your children. Talk about them when you sit at home and when you walk along the road, when you lie down and when you get up.* We impress them on our children by talking about these things all the time. I don't mean sermonizing from morning to night, but living in the vitality of the joy and thankfulness of a child of God, seeing the goodness of his ways and keeping his truth on the front burner all the time.

Remember the wonderful promise of James 3:8, "come near to God and he will come near to you."

CHAPTER 12

Childhood—Goals
and Methods

THE BIG IDEA

Parents of school age children are confronted with new challenges. The children are spending more time away from the direct supervision of mother or father. Since you cannot be with him all the time, you must build on those early lessons of being under a person of authority. The big lesson for these middle years is character development. He must know what to do in hundreds of situations that you cannot anticipate. He needs biblical wisdom. His conscience must be developed as the reasoning factor of the soul so that he will know what he ought to do even when you are not there. We must appeal to the child's conscience, helping him to develop the capacity to reason to right conclusions using the Scriptures as his guide.

It is obvious that character development is not taught through the same methods as teaching a toddler to be under authority. Spanking works well to teach young children to obey, but is not effective at teaching a ten year old to be wise. We must address the heart using all the means of communication discussed in chapters 8–10 of *Shepherding a Child's Heart*.

This chapter discusses the information found in Chapters 16 & 17 of *Shepherding a Child's Heart*.

DIGGING INTO THE WORD

What do we mean by character development? What passages of Scripture describe these character development goals? Generate a list of character development goals from the following passages.

Exodus 20:1–17
Matthew 5:3–10
Romans 12:3–21
Galatians 5:22–23
Colossians 3:12–14
2 Peter 1:5–7

Leviticus 19:11–18
Romans 5:3–4
1 Corinthians 13:4–8
Ephesians 4:32
Philippians 2:3–4
James 3:17–19

1. List character development goals from the passages above:

_____

_____

_____

_____

_____

_____

_____

_____

_____

_____

_____

_____

You have probably noted that the character goals generated from these passages are rooted in true faith in the Lord Jesus Christ. Where does this leave us, if our children do not believe? Think of it this way. Calling your children to be what they cannot be fully and honestly without the work of God is a means of showing them how much they need the work of Christ to change, transform and empower them. The law of God is the schoolmaster that leads to salvation (Galatians 3:23–25). Showing them what they ought to be will make their inability to be what they ought to be obvious—providing you with the opportunity to show both their need of Christ and the transforming power of grace.

2. The conscience is our ally in working with our children. Make notes about the conscience from the following passages of Scripture.

1 Samuel 24:1–7 _____

_____

Romans 2:15 _____

_____

Romans 13:1–5 _____

_____

2 Corinthians 4:2 _____

_____

1 Peter 3:16 _____

_____

1 Timothy 4:2 _____

_____

Titus 1:15 _____

_____

3. As we seek to develop godly character in our children and appeal to their conscience in our instruction, we must communicate wisely and well. Note principles of godly communication from the following passages:

Proverbs 10:11 _____

_____

Proverbs 10:19–21 _____

_____

Proverbs 10:32 _____

_____

Proverbs 12:14 _____

_____

Proverbs 12:18 _____

_____

Proverbs 13:3 _____

_____

Proverbs 15:1–2 _____

_____

Proverbs 15:28 _____

_____

Proverbs 25:11 _____

_____

Proverbs 29:20 _____

_____

APPLICATION

1. Use the character development goals from the section above to generate some character development goals for your children. List areas in which you wish to see them develop. Think of the passages of Scripture to which you might turn. Think through ways to illustrate the need for character growth in specific areas. Follow the paradigm shown below.

Growth area:_____

_____

Passage(s) of Scripture:_____

_____

_____

Illustrations of need for this growth: _____

_____

_____

_____

How to open up the conversation: _____

_____

_____

_____

2. Chapter 16 of *Shepherding a Child's Heart* provides a three-pronged tool of diagnosis to help you understand your kids and their needs. Sit down with your spouse and think about your children in terms of the following categories:

A. Relationship with God

- Is there a conscious need for God?
- Is knowing and loving God important?
- Is God a source of strength and comfort?
- What choices reflect knowing God?
- Are God's ways and truth important?
- Do spiritual realities seem to matter?
- Is there an independent relationship with God?
- Does he talk about God?
- How does she talk about God?
- Is God grand or small?
- Is God a friend or judge; helper or taskmaster?
- Does she live as someone who is complete in Christ?

B. Relationship to himself

- How does he think of himself?
- Does he understand himself?
- Is he aware of personal strengths and weaknesses?
- Does he understand his personality?
- Is he confident or shy and diffident?
- Is he arrogant or humble?
- Is he chained by fears?
- Is he able to enjoy others?
- Does he feel superior or inferior to others?
- Is he able to work on his own?
- Does he need external props to stay on task?
- How much does he need the approbation of others?

C. Relationship with others

- How does he interact with others?
- Can he converse without making the conversation about himself?

- What does he bring out in others?
- Does he control others?
- Is he under other's control?
- Does he fawn for attention?
- Is he pleasant with kids his age?
- How does he deal with disappointment with people?
- Is he forgiving?
- Does he harbor bitterness toward others?
- How does he respond to being sinned against?
- What are his relationship strengths?
- What are his relationship weaknesses?

STRATEGIC QUESTIONS

The child rearing emphasis in this section is nurture rather than merely controlling and constraining behavior. We are good activities directors, sports organizers and social planners. Parents in our culture are not good at nurturing relationships. The things outlined above and in chapters 16 and 17 of *Shepherding a Child's Heart* are skills that must be developed.

1. What are the ways you must change in order to do the things described in this section?

_____

_____

_____

_____

_____

_____

Addressing the heart necessitates thinking clearly and thoroughly about the "what", "when", and "why" of behavior. Sometimes the fact that we do not think clearly about these things is reflected in asking poor questions of our children. For example, "why did you . . ." is usually a poor question. Here are some better questions for helping your children express a clearer understanding of their actions and responses.

- Tell me about the situation. . .
- How did you respond internally when . . .
- What did you do (or say)?
- What were you trying to accomplish in doing (saying) that?
- Did you accomplish what you wished?
- How did it help or hurt?
- What would have been a better thing to do (say)?
- Where was God in your thinking at the time?
- What could you have done to reflect the two great commands? (Matthew 22:37–40)

2. What questions could you add to this list?

_____

_____

_____

_____

_____

_____

_____

_____

_____

3. How would these questions be more beneficial to your child than your usual procedure in a similar situation?

_____

_____

_____

_____

_____

_____

Many times parents have desires that get in the way of nurturing their children. These desires are often plausible, but they become idols of the heart that distort your vision as you shepherd your children. Among those desires you might find:

- You want to be respected
- You want comfort
- You want appreciation
- You want success
- You want control
- You want ease
- You want peace

4. You want . . . what can you add to the list?

_____

_____

_____

_____

_____

_____

5. Think through some of the ways these things get in the ways of your shepherding of your kids.

_____

_____

_____

_____

_____

_____

_____

6. What are the commitments to change that you must make if you are going to be a nurturer of children rather than a activities director, sports organizer and social planner?

_____

_____

_____

_____

_____

_____

_____

_____

_____

_____

CONCLUDING THOUGHTS

God, the nurturing heavenly Father, places his children in situations in which their character is developed and they grow into maturity in Him. One of the contexts for nurture that he gives you is the experience of rearing children. All that he is to us as a Father becomes the source of strength, confidence and empowerment for us in this task that would otherwise be overwhelming.

Many passages remind us of our riches in Christ and the joy and confidence that is ours as we know this growth in our great God.

Look at Isaiah 12 and note the things about God and his redemption that fill you with confidence and joy in this task.

_____

_____

_____

_____

_____

_____

_____

_____

_____

_____

_____

_____

_____

CHAPTER 13

Teens—Goals and Methods

THE BIG IDEA

There is a great deal of complexity to shepherding kids through the teen years. The kids themselves are insecure and unstable, often influenced by a culture that is not easily quarantined. Parents are commonly both fearful and unsure about how to proceed. These are years in which many parents live in fear and dread of problems, both actual and potential. Many Christian parents disengage. They give up on the idea of being a nurturing influence in the life of their teen. They fail to see that the opportunity to shepherd is found in the problems that arise. All the issues that require parental correction, direction and involvement are opportunities for understanding and embracing our teens. Rather than living in fear and dread of these years, we must see them as years tailor-made for shepherding ministry. All the hopes, fear, aspirations, questions, doubts, goals and dreams of our teens are opportunities to shepherd their hearts. What our kids need is not rejection and stiffer rules; what they need is steady loving and gracious shepherding.

This chapter discusses the information found in Chapters 18 & 19 of *Shepherding a Child's Heart*.

DIGGING INTO THE WORD

Chapter 18 of *Shepherding a Child's Heart* presents three foundations for the teen years. We will revisit those here.

The Fear of the Lord

> The fear of the LORD is the beginning of knowledge, but fools despise wisdom and discipline.   *Proverbs 1:7*

Modern evangelicalism emphasizes the immanence of God—God with us, God our friend and companion—almost to the exclusion of the transcendence of God—God as holy, powerful, glorious and excellent beyond description. The result is that children raised in this environment frequently have no sense of the glory of God.

1. Look at the following passages of Scripture and generate a list of the ways your teenager will benefit from knowing the fear of the Lord.

Job 28:28 _____

Psalm 19:9 _____

Psalm 34:11–12 _____

Psalm 111:10 _____

Proverbs 1:7 _____

Proverbs 9:10 _____

Proverbs 10:27 _____

Proverbs 14:27 _____

Proverbs 15:33 _____

Proverbs 16:6 _____

Proverbs 19:23 _____

Proverbs 22:4 _____

Ecclesiastes 8:13_____

Ecclesiastes12:13 _____

Isaiah 33:6_____

Adherence to Parental Instruction

> Listen, my son, to your father's instruction and do not forsake your mother's teaching. They will be a garland to grace your head and a chain to adorn your neck.
>
> *Proverbs 1:8–9*

The father here is his own advocate. He is urging on his son the importance of parental instruction and guidance. In our culture young people don't feel the need for this sort of help. The culture encourages emancipation and independence. You must become skilled at helping your teens to see the benefits of adhering to the things that you have modeled and taught.

2. What other passages of Scripture emphasize remembering your parent's words?

_____

_____

_____

_____

_____

_____

Disassociation from the wicked

> My son, if sinners entice you, do not give in to them.
>
> *Proverbs 1:10*

Your teens will face the enticement of the wicked. Sinners will seek to interest them in drugs, illicit sex, pornography, alcohol and all manner of evil. The sinners who entice your kids will not be old men in trench coats with moles on their faces. They will be young people who come into your home, and who may even call you Mr. and Mrs.

3. Note how these passages warn against association with the wicked.

Psalm 1:1–6 _____

Psalm 9:16 _____

Psalm 10:4 _____

Psalm 11:5–6 _____

Psalm 32:10 _____

Psalm 37 _____

Psalm 55:23 _____

Psalm 141:4 _____

Psalm 145:20 _____

Psalm 147:6 _____

Proverbs 3:33 _____

Proverbs 4:14 _____

Proverbs 4:19 _____

Proverbs 5:22 _____

Proverbs 10:6–7 _____

Proverbs 10:24–30 _____

Proverbs 11:21 _____

Proverbs 11:23 _____

Proverbs 12:5–7 _____

Proverbs 14:32 _____

Proverbs 15:3 _____

Proverbs 15:8–9 _____

Proverbs 21:19 _____

Proverbs 22:5 _____

Proverbs 24:1 _____

Proverbs 24:19–20 _____

Proverbs 25:26 _____

Proverbs 28:4 _____

Proverbs 29:7 _____

Proverbs 29:16 _____

Proverbs 29:27 _____

What you must do is design some winsome way of using all this biblical data to persuade your teen of the dangers that track with association with the wicked.

APPLICATION

All the biblical principles of communication that we studied in Chapters 6–8 of this Parent Handbook apply when dealing with teens. All of your interaction must be done in a manner that makes your wisdom attractive. Angry, threatening parents are a poor advertisement for wisdom. They confirm the teen's suspicion that Mom and Dad really don't have anything of value to say.

Galatians 6:1–2 provides a nice paradigm for understanding how to engage your teens in constructive ways:

> Brothers, if someone is caught in a sin, you who are spiritual should restore him gently. But watch yourself, or you also may be tempted. Carry each other's burdens, and in this way you will fulfill the law of Christ.

Let's note some key words here.

Caught—your teens get caught in sin. This is not to deny the volitional aspect of sin. They make choices. But there is a "caught in sin" aspect to it as well. Sin is deceitful (Hebrews 3:13) and sin ensnares. Your children get "caught in sin" because they have accepted and believed the hollow and deceptive philosophies of this world. Your task is to help them see that they have been caught in sin.

Restore—your teens who have been "caught in sin" need restoration. The essential ministry is positive, not negative. You must move toward them as a restoration expert, not as a demolition crew. The objective is the positive objective of restoration.

Gently—Paul adds this adjective to describe how the restoration process must take place. Restoration work requires patience and gentleness. You can make the mistake of thinking that if you get mad enough and get in your teen's face, then you will accomplish your goals. You may get the teen's attention, but you have forgotten that a gentle tongue can break a bone. (Proverbs 22:5). Remember, your teens will never respond properly to life because you got mad enough to put them in their place (James 1:19–20).

Watch—This passage reminds you that even when you are restoring your teens you must be guarding your own heart. You must restore with a humility that acknowledges your own capacity to sin in any way that your teen sins. That realization humbles you and keeps you from self-righteousness that will hypocritically distance you from your teen and keep you from any ministry of restoration.

Carry—It is easy for you to feel like you do not have the time and should not have to be bothered with time consuming shepherding at this stage of the game. After all, your child is a teen, they should know and understand by now. You are reminded in this passage that we are called to carry one another's burdens. You are called to the task of being a carrier during this season of life.

STRATEGIC QUESTIONS

1. Colossians 3:16 says, "Let the Word of Christ dwell in you richly as you teach and admonish one another with all wisdom . . ." What are some things you can do to engage in solid Bible study with your teen so that he can see the wisdom and vitality of the Word of God?

_____

_____

_____

_____

_____

_____

Suggested study topics:

- Courtship and Dating
- Sexuality
- Relationships
- Friendship
- Teen years as preparation for life
- Developing wisdom and discernment

2. If the attraction of association with wicked teens is belonging and camaraderie, what can you do to insure that your home is a place to belong?

_____

_____

_____

_____

_____

_____

3. What are some fun things and activities you can do with your teen to insure that every contact with your teen is not just business? What can you look forward to doing together?

_____

_____

_____

_____

_____

_____

4. Every parent of a teen has been in conversations in which he has become emotional and upset. What are some ways you and your spouse can signal to each other and encourage each other to disengage temporarily when things are heating up?

_____

_____

_____

_____

_____

_____

_____

5. Critique your style of parenting your teen to discern ways that you respond that are not helpful and never bear good fruit. Ask your spouse for constructive help.

_____

_____

_____

_____

_____

_____

_____

_____

_____

CONCLUDING THOUGHTS

For this reason, since the day we heard about you, we have not stopped praying for you and asking God to fill you with the knowledge of his will through all spiritual wisdom and understanding. And we pray this in order that you may live a life worthy of the Lord and may please him in every way: bearing fruit in every good work, growing in the knowledge of God, being strengthened with all power according to his glorious might so that you may have great endurance and patience, and joyfully giving thanks to the Father, who has qualified you to share in the inheritance of the saints in the kingdom of light. *Colossians 1:9–12*

This prayer of the Apostle Paul for the Colossian church can be your prayer for yourself as the parent of teens. Meditate on some of these phrases, making notes about your prayers for yourself.

- asking God to fill you with the knowledge of his will through all spiritual wisdom and understanding.
- that you may live a life worthy of the Lord
- and may please him in every way:
- bearing fruit in every good work,
- growing in the knowledge of God
- being strengthened with all power according to his glorious might
- so that you may have great endurance
- and patience
- and joyfully giving thanks to the Father,
- who has qualified you to share in the inheritance of the saints in the kingdom of light.

This passage reminds us that all we need to do this task of shepherding the hearts of our children is found in God and his grace and enabling power.